Alcohol Issues

Editor: Tracy Biram

Volume 397

First published by Independence Educational Publishers
The Studio, High Green
Great Shelford
Cambridge CB22 5EG
England

Copyright

Photocopy licence

ISBN-13: 978 1 86168 855 2

Printed in Great Britain
Zenith Print Group

Contents

Introduction

Alcohol Issues is Volume 397 in the **issues** series. The aim of the series is to offer current, diverse information about important issues in our world, from a UK perspective.

ABOUT ALCOHOL

With the majority of Brits having had their first taste of alcohol before the legal drinking age of 18, this book explores the reasons why young people may drink. It also looks at the effects that alcohol has on the body and mind, and the dangers of drinking, from addiction to drink-spiking.

OUR SOURCES

Titles in the **issues** series are designed to function as educational resource books, providing a balanced overview of a specific subject.

The information in our books is comprised of facts, articles and opinions from many different sources, including:

- Newspaper reports and opinion pieces
- Website factsheets
- Magazine and journal articles
- Statistics and surveys
- Government reports
- Literature from special interest groups.

A NOTE ON CRITICAL EVALUATION

Because the information reprinted here is from a number of different sources, readers should bear in mind the origin of the text and whether the source is likely to have a particular bias when presenting information (or when conducting their research). It is hoped that, as you read about the many aspects of the issues explored in this book, you will critically evaluate the information presented.

It is important that you decide whether you are being presented with facts or opinions. Does the writer give a biased or unbiased report? If an opinion is being expressed, do you agree with the writer? Is there potential bias to the 'facts' or statistics behind an article?

ASSIGNMENTS

In the back of this book, you will find a selection of assignments designed to help you engage with the articles you have been reading and to explore your own opinions. Some tasks will take longer than others and there is a mixture of design, writing and research-based activities that you can complete alone or in a group.

FURTHER RESEARCH

At the end of each article we have listed its source and a website that you can visit if you would like to conduct your own research. Please remember to critically evaluate any sources that you consult and consider whether the information you are viewing is accurate and unbiased.

Useful Websites

www.ahauk.org
www.alcoholchange.org.uk
www.alcoholeducationtrust.org
www.brake.org.uk
www.cancerresearchuk.org
www.helpmestop.org.uk
www.ias.org.uk
www.independent.co.uk
www.nhs.uk
www.ons.gov.uk
www.rehab4addiction.co.uk
www.talktofrank.co.uk
www.telegraph.co.uk
www.theconversation.com
www.thenorthernecho.co.uk
www.topdoctors.co.uk
www.ucl.ac.uk
www.walesonline.co.uk
www.yougov.co.uk
www.youngpeopleshealth.org.uk

Chapter 1 About Alcohol

Alcohol

Quick info

How the drug works varies from person to person

How you might feel

Sociable, chatty, relaxed and/or anxious, aggressive, risk-taking.

Effects on your body

Too much alcohol can mean slurred speech, blurred vision, loss of balance/coordination.

How long it takes to work

Effects kick in within about 10 minutes or so, depending on the strength of your drink and how fast you drink it.

How long the effects last

Can stay in your system for several hours - hangover next day.

Common risks

Binge drinking can lead to injuries from falls, accidents or assaults. Long-term effects include damage to the brain, body and organs. Mixing alcohol with benzos or other depressants can increase the risk of death.

How it looks, tastes and smells

What does it look like?

Alcohol comes in a wide range of drinks with different alcoholic strengths, colours and tastes. Alcohol often has labels with useful information, such as how many units are in the drink. All labels are required by law to display the strength of the drink (alcohol by volume, or ABV).

How do people take it?

What we mean by alcohol here is alcoholic drinks, such as beer, wine and spirits. The scientific name for the alcohol in these drinks is ethanol or ethyl alcohol.

Spirits usually contain a much higher concentration of alcohol than wine or lager and are normally drunk in smaller measures.

Ready-to-drink 'mixers' and 'alcopops' may not seem to be strong drinks but they may contain more alcohol than typical bottles or cans of beer or cider.

There is no completely safe level of drinking, but by sticking within these guidelines, you can lower your risk of harming your health.

To keep the risk of harm from alcohol low, men and women are advised not to regularly drink more than 14 units a week.

Don't 'save up' your units to use in one or two days. If you do drink as much as 14 units in a week you should spread this out over three or more days.

If you want to cut down how much you're drinking, a good way to help achieve this is to have several drink-free days each week.

If you are out for a drink, have something alcohol-free, every other drink.

Units of alcohol

A unit is a way of expressing the actual amount of pure alcohol that is in a drink. This allows you to compare how strong one type of alcoholic drink is to another type.

For example: 75cl Bottle of wine = approximately 10 units, 500 cl can of 4% lager = 2 units, 1 litre bottle of 40% spirits = 40 units

Check the label on drinks as they often show the total number of alcohol units in the can or bottle. If they don't, you can calculate the units by multiplying its ABV (ABV is 'alcohol by volume' that shows you the strength of an alcoholic drink), by the volume of the drink (in mls) and then dividing by 1,000.

How it feels

How does it make you feel?

Just enough can make you feel sociable; too much and you'll have a hangover the next day, and may not even remember what you got up to; and way too much alcohol in a single session could put you in a coma or even kill you.

Although it's legal for people aged 18 and over to buy and drink alcohol, that doesn't mean it's safe.

Some effects include: Reduced feelings of anxiety and inhibitions, which can help you feel more sociable. An exaggeration of whatever mood you're in when you start drinking.

Drinking a lot of alcohol (more than 6-8 units) will make you intoxicated (drunk), which will show itself as increasingly: slurred speech; lack of co-ordination and blurred vision.

Alcohol raises testosterone levels in males and females, which affects both sexual drive and aggression.

The more you drink in a sitting, the more your judgement will be affected, and this can lead to doing things or taking risks that you otherwise wouldn't.

Duration

How long the effects last and the drug stays in your system depends on how much you've taken, your size, whether you've eaten and what other drugs you may have also taken.

How quickly you feel the effects and how long they last, depend on how much you've taken and how quickly, your size, whether you've eaten and any other drugs you may have also taken.

Alcohol is broken down by the liver into other compounds at the rate of about 1 unit per hour. Only the liver breaks down alcohol in the body and nothing else, such as drinking coffee or caffeine drinks, will speed that process up, though you may feel more alert.

The short-term effects of alcohol can last for a day or two, depending on how much you drank, including any hangover.

Alcohol and the compounds that alcohol is broken down into by your liver are poisonous and although they are eventually excreted from the system, they have a potentially damaging effect on almost every system of the body, which can result in health damage over time.

The risks

Physical health risks

Drinking alcohol causes a wide range of physical and mental health problems, either because of binge drinking or from regularly drinking more than 14 units per week.

Binge drinking can lead to injuries from falls, accidents or assaults. Drinking above the low risk guidelines on a regular basis can cause illnesses such as depression, high blood pressure, stroke, liver disease, cancers of the throat, mouth breast and liver.

Alcohol contributes to all kinds of problems in Britain, from violent crime to domestic violence to car-related deaths to missing work and unemployment.

There are short-term risks like injuries and accidents which can happen because of being drunk. These can include head injuries, scars, and can sometimes be fatal. There are other short-term risks such as alcohol poisoning.

Long-term risks come from regularly drinking alcohol over the low risk guideline over a long time. Then the risks of getting different diseases increase and can lead to illnesses, such as cancer, stroke, heart disease, liver disease, and damage to your brain and nervous system.

Long-term effects include damage to the brain, body and its organs. This can take years to develop and can lead to a wide range of serious health problems, like cancers, that you may not realise are due to alcohol.

Other chemical forms of alcohol, such as methanol (meths), isopropanol and butanol, are much more toxic than ethanol and should not be consumed by humans.

Counterfeit alcohol

The scientific name for the alcohol in drinks is ethanol or ethyl alcohol. Other types of alcohol, such as methanol and butanol, are much more toxic than ethanol and should not be consumed by humans, as they can cause severe liver damage, blindness and even death.

Although counterfeit alcoholic drinks may contain these toxic forms of alcohol or other poisonous impurities, the vast majority of alcohol brought from legitimate sources will not.

Counterfeit alcoholic drinks tend to be sold in places you wouldn't normally buy alcohol, such as car boot sales, and sold at low prices. Sometimes, a clue to knowing that an alcoholic drink is counterfeit is its labelling and packing – there may be spelling mistakes, holographic labels aren't holographic, etc.

'Alcopops' and ready-to-drink 'mixers' may not seem to be strong drinks but they may contain more alcohol than typical bottles or cans of beer or cider.

Mixing

Is it dangerous to mix with other drugs?

Alcoholic drinks are often mixed with non-alcoholic drinks (mixers), such as fruit juice, tonic water or lemonade, to give different flavours. This means there is more liquid in the drink but doesn't reduce the amount of alcohol in the whole drink. So whether you drink a unit of vodka on its own or with 25cl of lemonade, you are still drinking a unit of vodka.

Mixing alcohol with mixers does increase the overall volume of the drink, which means it takes longer to drink, so that you might not have as many drinks in a session. Adding the mixer to the alcoholic drink, rather than adding the alcohol to the mixer, makes it easier to gauge the amount of alcohol in your glass. Drinking spirits or wine straight from the bottle makes it much more difficult to gauge how many units you are drinking.

Mixing different types of alcoholic drinks together e.g. cider and lager as a 'Snakebite' doesn't multiply the effect of the alcohol.

Any time you mix alcohol and other drugs together you take on new risks. Things that affect your risk include how much you have been drinking, the type of drug, the strength and how much you take.

It is particularly dangerous to mix alcohol with depressants such as benzodiazepine - Xanax and Valium are linked with deaths from overdose.

Alcohol and cocaine together can be particularly dangerous. Once they mix together in the body they produce a toxic chemical called cocaethylene, which can cause heart problems, stroke and liver damage.

Cocaethylene stays in the body much longer than cocaine or alcohol alone, and this increases the damage done to the heart and liver.

Addiction

Can you get addicted?

Can you get addicted? Some people's drinking gradually gets out of control and if they regularly drink a lot, alcohol can become overly important in their lives. Losing control of drinking is known as alcohol dependence, which leads to particularly high risk of harming their health.

Dependence on alcohol can creep up on you. Your tolerance to alcohol gradually increases the more you drink and the more often you drink, so you may find that over time you need more alcohol to get the same effect, you may seem to be getting better at holding your drink when that's really a sign of a developing problem. This problem may get more severe as you drink more and more regularly.

People who are more dependent on alcohol may have withdrawal symptoms if they stop drinking suddenly and these can be severe. In some cases the withdrawal symptoms can be fatal, so a person may require medical treatment because of this risk of death. Typically, the symptoms include sweating, shaking, nausea and retching and high levels of anxiety. Some people can develop hallucinations or fits, or occasionally life-threatening delirious states. In these cases, it can be very dangerous to stop drinking suddenly without medical supervision.

Anyone who experiences these severe symptoms when they stop drinking should seek medical attention immediately. It is safer for them to drink some alcohol to control the withdrawal than to suffer the symptoms without medical support.

Drinking heavily over several years can result in alcohol-related liver disease. Because the liver has no nerves, people are often unaware that they are developing liver disease until it's quite advanced. A first outward sign might be jaundice, when the skin or whites of the eyes turn yellow. If someone develops jaundice, it's important that they get urgent medical care.

The law

Class: Legal

Additional law details

It's against the law for anyone under 18 to buy alcohol in a pub, off-licence or supermarket or online.

Anyone over 18 can buy and drink alcohol legally in licensed premises in Britain. But, a lot of shops operate a scheme called Challenge 21 where if you look under 21 (or 25 in some places) and don't have proof of your age they will refuse to sell you alcohol.

Children aged under 16 must be accompanied by an adult in a pub or bar.

The police have the power to stop a person and confiscate alcohol in a public place if they reasonably suspect the person to be aged under 18. Young people under 18 who persistently drink or are found possessing alcohol in public places may be prosecuted.

It's illegal to give an alcoholic drink to a child under 5 except in certain circumstances (such as under medical supervision).

It's illegal for an adult to buy alcohol for someone aged under 18, except where that person buys beer, wine or cider for someone aged 16 or 17 to be drunk with a table meal while accompanied by a person over 18.

It's illegal to drive with more than 80 milligrams per 100 millilitres of blood in your system. People absorb alcohol at different rates and it's difficult to judge how many drinks would put you over this legal limit, so because any amount of alcohol slows down reaction times, it's safest not to drink at all before driving

Official guidelines

The UK Chief Medical Officers advise that an alcohol-free childhood is the healthiest and best option. However, if young people drink alcohol:

- It should not be until at least the age of 15 years.
- If young people aged 15 to 17 years consume alcohol, it should always be with the guidance of a parent or carer or in a supervised environment.
- Parents and young people should be aware that drinking, even at 15 or older, can be hazardous to health and that not drinking is the healthiest option for young people.
- If 15- to 17-year-olds do consume alcohol, they should do so infrequently and certainly on no more than one day a week.
- Young people aged 15 to 17 years should never exceed recommended adult daily limits and, on days when they drink, consumption should usually be below these levels.
- Adults are safest not to drink regularly more than 14 units per week, to keep health risks from drinking alcohol to a low level. And if they do drink as much as 14 units per week, it is best to spread this evenly over 3 days or more. If they want to cut down the amount they're drinking, a good way to help achieve this is to have several drink-free days each week.

www.talktofrank.co.uk

Alcohol-specific deaths in the UK

Main points

- In 2019, there were 7,565 deaths registered in the UK that related to alcohol-specific causes, the second highest since the data time series began in 2001.
- The 2019 age-standardised alcohol-specific death rate was 11.8 deaths per 100,000 people, remaining stable with no significant change since last year.
- Since the beginning of the data time series in 2001, rates of alcohol-specific deaths for males have consistently been more than double those for females (16.1 and 7.8 deaths per 100,000 registered in 2019 respectively).
- Alcohol-specific death rates were highest among those aged 55 to 59 years and 60 to 64 years for both men and women in 2019.
- Northern Ireland and Scotland had the highest rates of alcohol-specific death in 2019 (18.8 and 18.6 deaths per 100,000 people respectively).
- Since 2001, the alcohol-specific death rate has risen significantly for both men and women in England and in Northern Ireland.

Alcohol-specific deaths in the UK

Rates of alcohol-specific deaths have remained stable in recent years.

There were 7,565 deaths related to alcohol-specific causes registered in the UK in 2019, equivalent to 11.8 deaths per 100,000 people; this is similar to the figures seen in 2018 when there were 7,551 registered deaths, equivalent to 11.9 deaths per 100,000 people.

Overall, rates of alcohol-specific deaths in the UK have remained stable in recent years, with no statistically significant differences in the year-on-year rates since 2012. Despite this, the 2019 rate is significantly higher than that observed at the beginning of the data time series in 2001, when there were 10.6 deaths per 100,000 population.

Rates of male alcohol-specific deaths are twice those of females

Over the course of the data time series, males have accounted for between 66.3% and 69.1% of all alcohol-specific deaths, and females between 30.9% and 33.7% of deaths. Taking population and age distribution into account, the latest rates in the UK were 16.1 (5,019 deaths) and 7.8 (2,546 deaths) per 100,000 people, for males and females respectively.

There have been significant increases since 2001 in the rate of alcohol-specific deaths in people aged 55 to 79 years

UK alcohol-specific deaths by age group show that in 2019 the highest rates for both men and women were among those aged 55 to 59 years and 60 to 64 years. For the 55 to 59 years age group the male death rate was 40.0 per 100,000 and for women it was 20.5 per 100,000, while the 60 to 64 years age group saw death rates of 40.7 and 19.1 for men and women respectively.

Over the course of the data time series between 2001 and 2019, there have been statistically significant increases in age-specific death rates for people aged 55 to 79 years. Changes in alcohol-specific death rates over time by age group in people are shown in Figure 2.

Figure 1: Rates of alcohol-specific deaths have increased by 11.3% since 2001

Age-standardised alcohol-specific death rates per 100,000 people, by sex; UK, deaths registered between 2001 and 2019

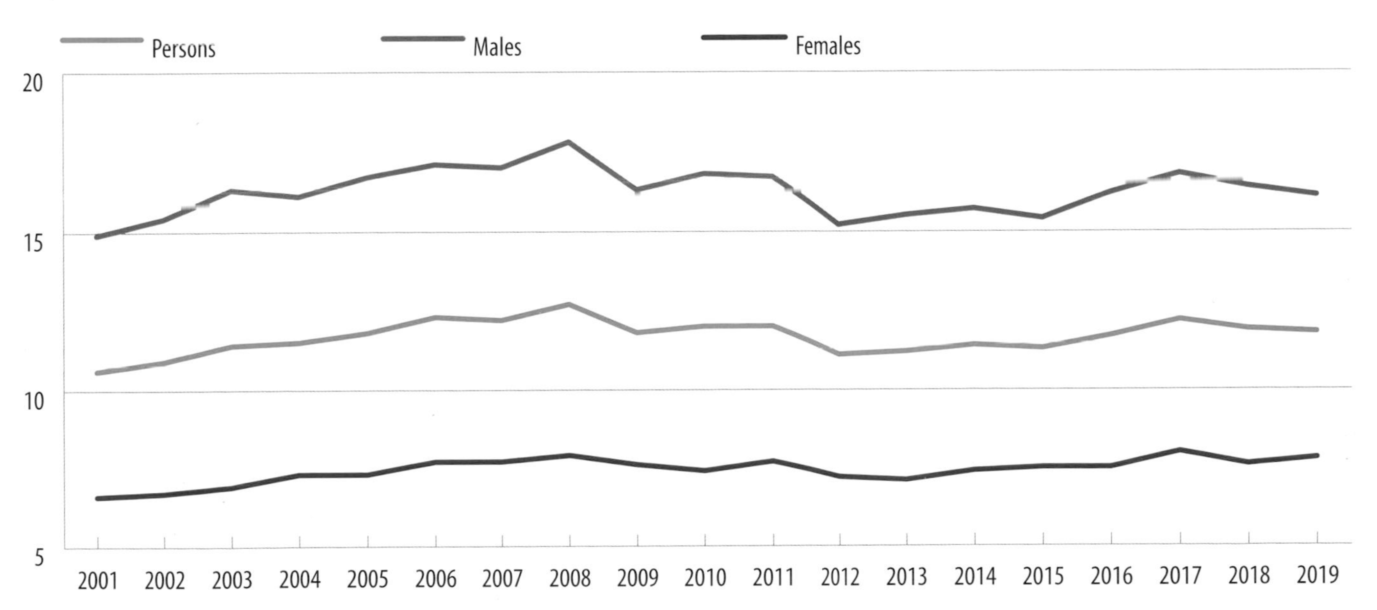

Notes:
Rates are expressed per 100,000 population and standardised to the 2013 European Standard Population.
Deaths of non-residents are included in figures for the UK.
Figures are for deaths registered in each calendar year.
Calculations are based on rounded figures.

Source: Office for National Statistics - Alcohol-specific deaths in the UK: registered in 2019, National Records of Scotland and Northern Ireland Statistics and Research Agency

Figure 2: In 2019, alcohol-specific death rates were highest among 55- to 59-year-olds and 60- to 64-year-olds

Age-specific alcohol-specific death rates per 100,000 people, by five-year age group; UK, deaths registered in 2001 and 2019

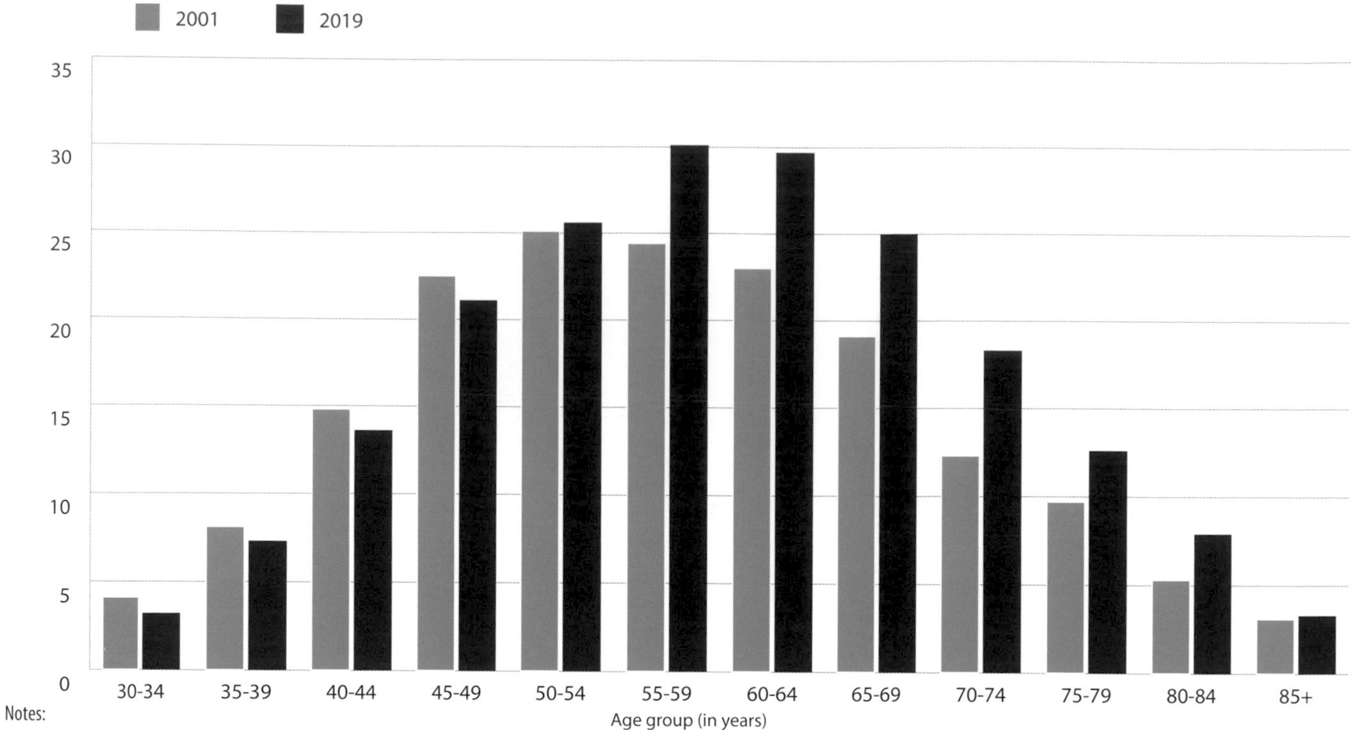

Notes:
1. Rates are expressed per 100,000 population.
2. Deaths of non-residents are included in figures for the UK.
3. Figures are for deaths registered in each calendar year.
4. Figures are for those aged 30 years and over as a result of small numbers of deaths in the younger age groups producing more statistical uncertainty.

Source: Office for National Statistics - Alcohol-specific deaths in the UK: registered in 2019, National Records of Scotland and Northern Ireland Statistics and Research Agency

The majority of alcohol-specific deaths are attributed to alcoholic liver disease

Given that the definition of alcohol-specific deaths includes mostly chronic conditions, such as alcoholic liver disease, the increased rates in the older age groups may be a consequence of misuse of alcohol that began years, or even decades, earlier. A third of alcohol-specific deaths in those aged under 30 years were caused by alcoholic liver disease in 2019, while more than three-quarters of alcohol-specific deaths in those aged over 30 years were from this condition.

The proportion of alcohol-specific deaths due to mental and behavioural disorders increased with age, reaching a high of 47.6% of alcohol-specific deaths in persons aged 85 to 89 years. The reverse is true for accidental poisoning by and exposure to alcohol, which accounted for 50.0% of alcohol-specific deaths in those aged 20 to 24 years and no more than 2.4% in those aged over 65 years.

Figure 3 shows the number of alcohol-specific deaths by five-year age group and the following three individual causes, which contributed 96.2% of all alcohol-specific deaths registered in 2019:

- alcoholic liver disease (International Classification of Diseases: ICD-10 code K70, 77.2% of alcohol-specific deaths)
- mental and behavioural disorders due to the use of alcohol (ICD-10 code F10, 12.7% of deaths)
- accidental poisoning by and exposure to alcohol (ICD-10 code X45, 6.4% of deaths)

High numbers of deaths due to the misuse of alcohol have been reported across Europe, with the European Commission reporting that about 800 people in Europe die from alcohol-attributable causes every single day (PDF, 498KB), and the World Health Organization reporting that across 30 European countries, 7.6 million years of life were lost prematurely in 2016 alone (PDF, 5.43MB).

Alcohol-specific deaths by UK constituent country

Northern Ireland was the UK constituent country with the highest alcohol-specific death rate in 2019 with 18.8 deaths per 100,000, however, the difference between Northern Ireland and Scotland in 2019 was not statistically significant. England and Wales continue to have lower rates of alcohol-specific deaths, with 10.9 and 11.8 deaths per 100,000 people respectively.

Since the beginning of the data time series in 2001, age-standardised rates of alcohol-specific deaths in Scotland have tended to be highest of the four UK constituent countries. Since peaking at 28.5 deaths per 100,000 in 2006, the alcohol-specific death rate has fallen by more than a third to 18.6 deaths per 100,000 in 2019. A minimum unit pricing policy was implemented by the Scottish Government on 1 May 2018. It is too early to measure the impact of this policy on mortality using the alcohol-specific definition, however, this will remain a point of interest in the future. Minimum pricing for alcohol was also introduced in Wales on 2 March 2020.

Scotland remains the only UK constituent country to show statistically significant improvement when comparing with

Figure 3: More than three-quarters of alcohol-specific deaths were caused by alcoholic liver disease

Numbers of alcohol-specific deaths, by five-year age group and individual cause; UK, deaths registered in 2019

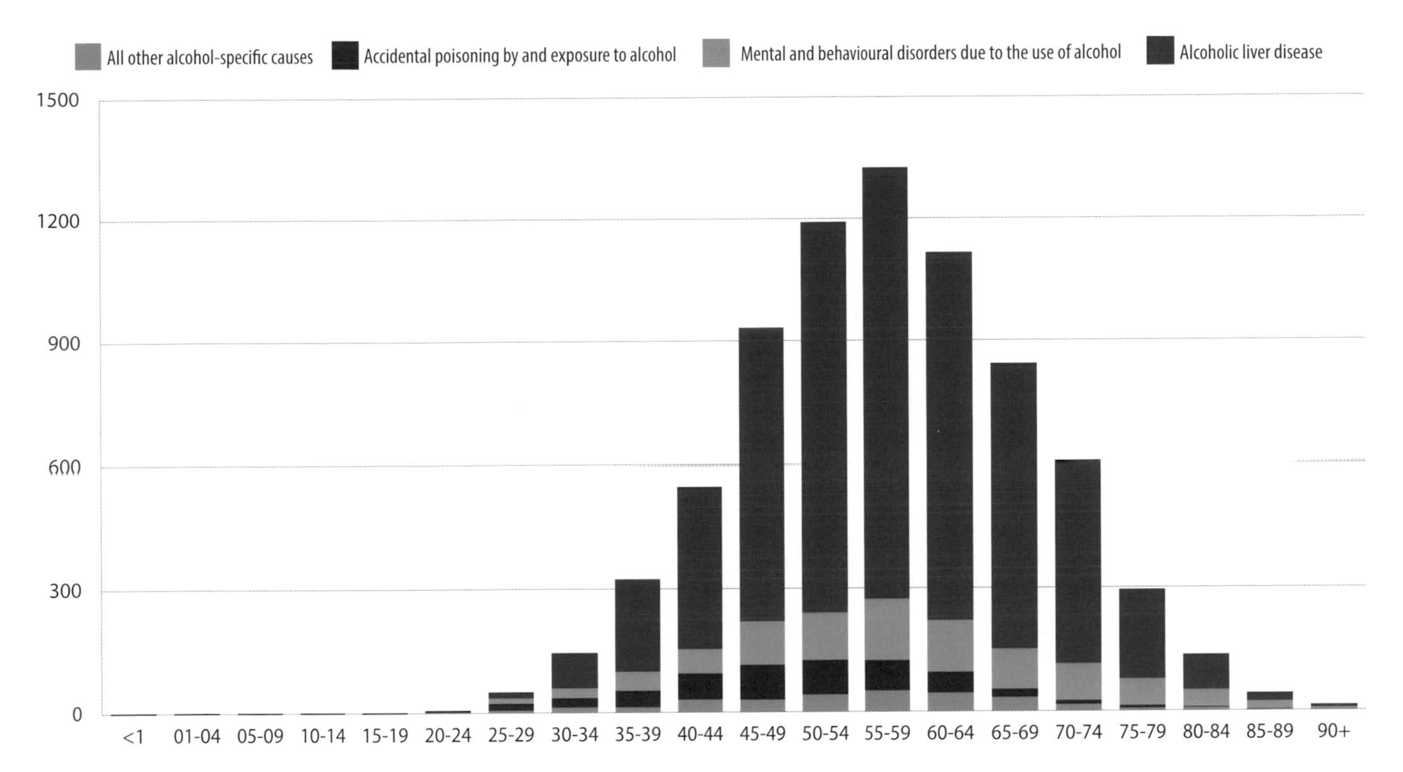

Notes:
1. Deaths of non-residents are included in figures for the UK.
2. Figures are for deaths registered in each calendar year.

Source: Office for National Statistics - Alcohol-specific deaths in the UK: registered in 2019, National Records of Scotland and Northern Ireland Statistics and Research Agency

Figure 4: Of the four UK constituent countries, rates of alcohol-specific deaths were highest in Northern Ireland in 2019

Age-standardised alcohol-specific death rates per 100,000 people; UK constituent countries, deaths registered between 2001 and 2019

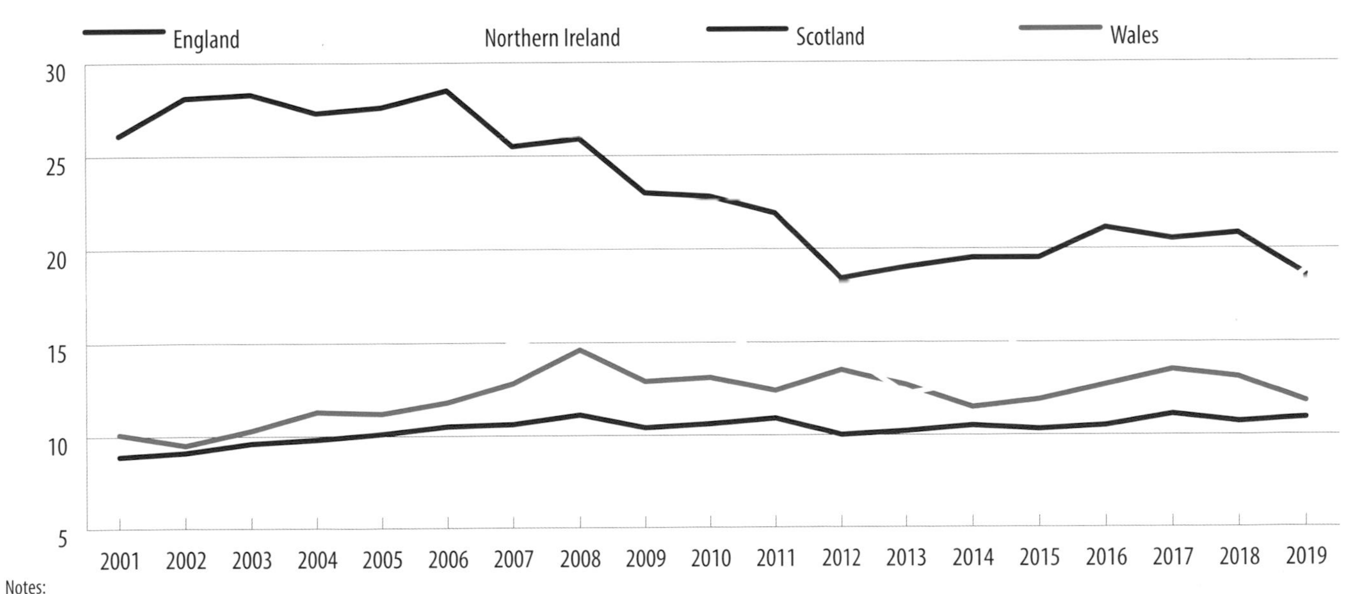

Notes:
1. Rates are expressed per 100,000 population and standardised to the 2013 European Standard Population.
2. Figures for Scotland and Northern Ireland include deaths of non-residents. However, figures for England and Wales (separately) exclude deaths of non-residents and are based on November 2020 boundaries.
3. Figures are for deaths registered in each calendar year.

Source: Office for National Statistics - Alcohol-specific deaths in the UK: registered in 2019, National Records of Scotland and Northern Ireland Statistics and Research Agency

2001 rates. In comparison, both England and Northern Ireland had statistically significant increases in the alcohol-specific death rate over the same period, while the increase seen in Wales was not statistically significant.

2 February 2021

www.ons.gov.uk

Does alcohol cause cancer?

Yes, alcohol can cause 7 different types of cancer.

It's alcohol itself that causes damage - what type of alcohol you drink doesn't matter.

Whatever your drinking habits, cutting down will reduce your risk.

What's my cancer risk from drinking alcohol?

If you drink alcohol, you are more likely to get cancer than if you don't. But drinking alcohol doesn't mean that you'll definitely get cancer. Your exact risk will depend on lots of factors, including things you can't change such as your age and genetics.

Cutting down on alcohol can help reduce the risk of cancer.

Even a small amount of alcohol can increase your risk, so the more you can cut down the more you can reduce your risk.

Drinking less alcohol has lots of other benefits too. You can reduce your risk of accidents, high blood pressure and liver disease by cutting back.

How does alcohol cause cancer?

There are three main ways alcohol can cause cancer:

- Damage to cells. When we drink alcohol, our bodies turn it into a chemical called acetaldehyde. Acetaldehyde can cause damage to our cells and can also stop the cells from repairing this damage.
- Changes to hormones. Alcohol can increase the levels of some hormones such as oestrogen and insulin. Hormones are chemical messengers and higher levels can make cells divide more often, which raises the chance that cancer cells will develop.
- Changes to cells in the mouth and throat. Alcohol can make cells in the mouth and throat more likely to absorb harmful chemicals. This makes it easier for cancer-causing substances (like those found in cigarette smoke) to get into the cell and cause damage.

Remember, it's the alcohol itself that causes damage. It doesn't matter whether you drink beer, wine or spirits. All types of alcoholic drink can cause cancer.

There's plenty of tricks that people claim 'cure' hangovers and reverse damage from alcohol. But even if they work for your hangover, they don't cancel out the damage from drinking alcohol.

What types of cancer does alcohol cause?

Drinking alcohol increases the risk of 7 different types of cancer. This includes:

- Breast and bowel cancer (two of the most common types).
- Mouth cancer.
- Some types of throat cancer: oesophagus (food pipe), larynx (voice box), and pharynx (upper throat).
- Liver cancer.

Alcohol and breast cancer

Breast cancer is the most common cancer in the UK and drinking alcohol is one of the biggest risk factors for breast cancer. Around 4,400 breast cancer cases each year are caused by drinking alcohol. The risk increases even at low levels of drinking.

Is binge drinking worse for me?

Binge drinking causes problems, but it's no worse for cancer risk than spreading drinks out across the week. No drinking pattern is worse than another. It's how much alcohol you drink that matters.

Drinking alcohol increases the risk of cancer whether you drink it all in one go or spread it throughout the week.

Are there any health benefits from drinking alcohol?

You may have heard that drinking alcohol can be good for the heart. But the NHS alcohol guidelines say that the evidence is not clear and that there is no completely safe level of drinking. You should not drink alcohol for health benefits. The risk of cancer increases even drinking small amounts of alcohol.

Is it worse if I drink and smoke?

Drinking alcohol is worse for you if you smoke. This is because tobacco and alcohol work together to cause much more damage to cells. This increases the risk of cancer.

For example, people who both smoke and drink alcohol are at a higher risk of mouth and upper throat cancer. This can happen because:

Alcohol may make it easier for harmful chemicals from tobacco smoke to pass through the mouth and throat into the bloodstream.

Alcohol may change how the toxic chemicals from tobacco smoke are broken down in the body, making them even more harmful.

31 March 2021

The above information is reprinted with kind permission from Cancer Research UK.

www.cancerresearchuk.org

Is alcohol really a drug?

By Tim Woodley

Is alcohol a drug like cannabis or cocaine? Should I treat it like one or is it 'different'? Is it safer or more dangerous? Clear to some, the fact remains that many adults in the UK have a limited understanding of the realities and dangers of heavy alcohol consumption.

First things first: Yes, alcohol is a drug – a dangerous one. Perceived as safer by many due to its legality and prevalence in popular media and binge drinking culture, alcohol is nevertheless a drug that kills thousands every year. Behind those deaths are the sad stories of families and social circles ripped apart and, in most cases, the bleak and private spiral of addiction.

This is even more worrying as nearly a third of people (29%) are reporting that they have drunk more alcohol than they normally would during COVID-19 lockdown, according to a major new study by the Policy Institute at King's College London in partnership with Ipsos MORI.

Colin Drummond, Professor of Addiction Psychiatry from the Institute of Psychiatry, Psychology & Neuroscience (IoPPN), King's College London said: 'There is extensive evidence that the population level of alcohol consumption is highly correlated with health harm. So, with a substantial increase in alcohol consumption during the COVID-19 pandemic as shown in the latest Ipsos MORI survey, we can expect in due course a surge in alcohol-related ill health including alcohol-related liver disease admissions and deaths.'

Understanding the basics

Alcohol is classified as a Central Nervous System (CNS) depressant. This refers to the way it operates in the body and the brain; the substance slows down how our brain operates, leading to the deterioration of other functions in the body. This happens due to the heightened production of GABA in the body. Gamma-aminobutyric acid is an inhibitory neurotransmitter and, when produced in large enough quantities when we drink heavily, it is what slows our other functions, providing the depressant effect.

Interestingly, however, alcohol also acts as a stimulant. When consumed in smaller amounts, these stimulatory effects are felt and are usually what is chased by drinkers. It's the stimulating side of alcohol that provides the positive feelings we enjoy from the drug, such as improvements in mood, heightened confidence and natural talkativeness. It's this aspect of the drug that also increases our blood pressure and heart rate when drinking.

The more we drink, the more we start to experience the depressant effects of alcohol over the stimulant effects. Some studies show that people who naturally experience more of the stimulant effects of the drug are more likely to become alcoholics. It's important to remember, though, that there are a number of other genetic and environmental factors that affect your likelihood to develop addiction. These can include pre-existing conditions like depression and addiction to other substances.

Why is alcohol addictive? How does that work?

We can understand addiction simply as the uncontrollable compulsion to consume alcohol at any cost – even if we're fully aware of the damaging consequences of doing so. Alcohol is addictive both psychologically and physically, releasing endorphins and dopamine in the brain upon use which gives us strong feelings of pleasure and euphoria.

Interestingly, our brain's ability to react to substances, our environment and our actions 'elastically' makes addiction more likely; heavy alcohol use can physically change its function and chemistry, overloading the reward centres repeatedly to cause cravings that reinforce bad drinking behaviours. Studies even show that some people naturally see their brains release more endorphins and dopamine than others when drinking, which makes them more susceptible to developing alcohol addiction via heavy use.

The causes of alcohol withdrawal

Alcohol affects multiple bodily functions that result in alcohol withdrawal when attempting to stop. First and foremost, excessive alcohol consumption agitates and irritates the central nervous system. Alcohol has a sedative effect on the brain in which it suppresses certain neurotransmitters, causing people to feel at ease after drinking. It is this effect when drinking that causes people to experience initial feelings of happiness, increased sociability, and relaxation.

In heavy long-term drinking, the brain is almost continuously exposed to the depressant effects of alcohol. This causes the person to develop a physical dependence on the substance. Once the body becomes dependent on alcohol, it requires more and more of the substance to produce the same effects. When someone abruptly quits drinking, the neurotransmitters are no longer inhibited by alcohol and the brain scrambles to adjust to the new chemical imbalance. This causes the most uncomfortable signs of withdrawal symptoms such as insomnia, rapid heartbeat, changes in blood pressure, sweating, tremors and fever.

Is alcohol withdrawal dangerous like with some other drugs?

Yes. Alcohol withdrawal symptoms can occur as early as two hours after your last drink. Typically, symptoms will peak within the first 24 to 48 hours upon cessation. While some people experience very few withdrawal symptoms, others may suffer from more serious side effects. Heavy drinkers who suddenly stop drinking may experience a range of dangerous symptoms which can include heart attacks and seizures which can lead to death, so it's important for those drinking heavily to undergo medically assisted detox.

Chris Cordell, Help Me Stop's General Manager, says 'Help Me Stop offers a free service which we can do face to face, over the phone or online where we can discuss someone's drinking and using recognised assessment tools advise if someone's drinking levels would indicate that they may need medical assistance In managing their withdrawals. In many instances a community detox is possible, but some will need an inpatient detox'.

For many people using alcohol problematically, withdrawal involves the steady weaning off from drinking over a short period of time, making the withdrawal process safer and less likely to induce seizures, heart attacks and other dangerous symptoms.

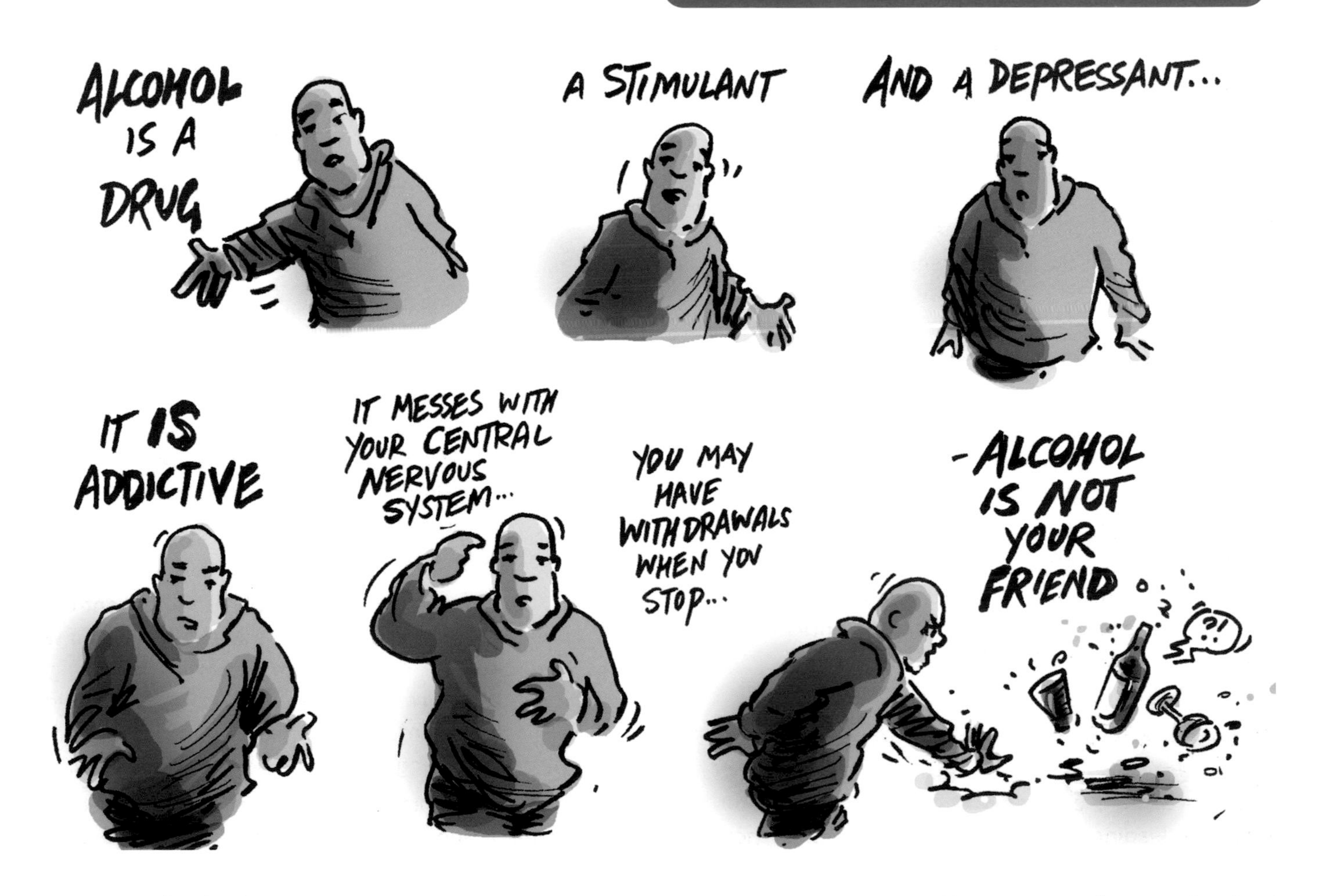

The risks of drinking too much

Regularly drinking more than 14 units of alcohol a week risks damaging your health.

The recommended weekly limit of 14 units is equivalent to 6 pints of average-strength beer or 10 small glasses of low-strength wine.

New evidence around the health harms from regular drinking have emerged in recent years.

There's now a better understanding of the link between drinking and some illnesses, including a range of cancers.

The previously held position that some level of alcohol was good for the heart has been revised.

It's now thought that the evidence on a protective effect from moderate drinking is less strong than previously thought.

Low-risk drinking advice

To keep health risks from alcohol to a low level if you drink most weeks:

- men and women are advised not to drink more than 14 units a week on a regular basis
- spread your drinking over 3 or more days if you regularly drink as much as 14 units a week
- if you want to cut down, try to have several drink-free days each week

If you're pregnant or think you could become pregnant, the safest approach is not to drink alcohol at all to keep risks to your baby to a minimum.

No 'safe' drinking level

If you drink less than 14 units a week, this is considered low-risk drinking.

It's called 'low risk' rather than 'safe' because there's no safe drinking level.

The type of illnesses you can develop after 10 to 20 years of regularly drinking more than 14 units a week include:

- cancers of the mouth, throat and breast
- stroke
- heart disease
- liver disease
- brain damage
- damage to the nervous system

There's also evidence that regular drinking at high-risk levels can make your mental health worse.

Research has found strong links between alcohol misuse and self-harming, including suicide.

The effects of alcohol on your health will depend on how much you drink. The less you drink, the lower the health risks.

'Single session' drinking

Drinking too much too quickly on any single occasion can increase your risk of:

- accidents resulting in injury, causing death in some cases
- misjudging risky situations
- losing self-control, like having unprotected sex or getting involved in violence

To reduce your health risks on any single session:

- limit how much you drink
- drink more slowly
- drink with food
- alternate with water or non-alcoholic drinks

23 May 2019

What is binge drinking?

Binge drinking usually refers to drinking lots of alcohol in a short space of time or drinking to get drunk.

In the UK, binge drinking is drinking more than:

- 8 units of alcohol in a single session for men
- 6 units of alcohol in a single session for women

Examples:

- 6 units is 2 pints of 5% strength beer or 2 large (250ml) glasses of 12% wine
- 8 units is 5 bottles (330ml) of 5% strength beer or 5 small (125ml) glasses of 13% wine

This is not an exact definition for binge drinking that applies to everyone, as tolerance to alcohol can vary from person to person.

The speed of drinking in a session can also alter alcohol's effects.

Drinking too much, too quickly on a single occasion can increase your risk of:

- accidents resulting in injury, causing death in some cases
- misjudging risky situations
- losing self-control, like having unprotected sex

How to reduce your risk

To reduce your health risk from binge drinking, try to:

- limit how much you drink on any single occasion
- drink more slowly
- drink with food
- alternate with water or non-alcoholic drinks
- plan ahead to avoid problems, such as making sure you can get home safely or having people you trust with you

Keeping track of your drinking is even more important if you're out in risky or unfamiliar circumstances.

You can be at risk from others, and may not be able to look after your friends.

You can easily lose control of what you do or say and may make risky decisions, thinking you're invulnerable.

How alcohol affects you drink by drink

Below is a drink-by-drink guide, based on a standard (175ml) 13% volume glass of white wine and 4% strength pint of lager, showing how quickly alcohol can affect your mind and body.

1 glass of white wine or a pint of lager (just over 2 units):

- You're talkative and feel relaxed.
- Your self-confidence increases.
- Driving ability is already impaired, which is why it's best to drink no alcohol if you're driving.

2 glasses of white wine or 2 pints of lager (just over 4 units):

- Your blood flow increases.
- You feel less inhibited and your attention span is shorter.
- You start dehydrating, one of the causes of a hangover.

3 glasses of white wine or 3 pints of lager (just under 7 units):

- Your reaction time is slower.
- Your liver has to work harder.
- Your sex drive may increase, while your judgement may decrease.

4 glasses of white wine or 4 pints of lager (just over 9 units):

- You're easily confused.
- You're noticeably emotional.
- Your sex drive could now decrease and you may become less capable.

Bear in mind that some people, including women, young people and those with smaller builds, may experience the effects after drinking smaller amounts of alcohol.

If you find you have become tolerant to the effects of alcohol, you may be at risk of health problems.

In that case, consider whether it's time to cut back on your drinking or you need to seek help.

How to reduce your risk from alcohol

To keep health risks from alcohol to a low level if you drink most weeks:

- men and women are advised not to drink more than 14 units a week on a regular basis
- spread your drinking over 3 or more days if you regularly drink as much as 14 units a week
- if you want to cut down, try to have several drink-free days each week

Fourteen units is equivalent to 6 pints of 4% beer or 6 glasses (175ml) of 13% wine.

15 February 2019

www.nhs.uk

Alcohol Awareness

Chapter 2

What makes a person an alcoholic?

Written by: Dr Lars Davidsson

Edited by: Cameron Gibson-Watt

There are several definitions of alcohol addiction that have changed over the years. Alcohol addiction can present itself in many different ways; it depends on the amount and how often you are drinking and the type of alcoholic drink you consume regularly. While some people drink heavily all day long, others binge drink and then stay sober for a while. Dr Lars Davidsson, a consultant psychiatrist at the Anglo European Clinic, gives us an overview of what an alcohol addiction exactly is and what the first steps in treating this condition involve.

What exactly is alcohol addiction?

Alcohol addiction can be hard to identify as drinking is a part of life for many people and is so widely accepted in our society. However, if you find you are drinking alcohol and it results in medical or social problems, then it's likely you have an alcohol problem. If you find people are complaining about your drinking habits, such as your friends, family or partner, and you find yourself in difficult situations frequently due to your drinking habits, then it might be the early signs of alcohol addiction. It is generally agreed that someone is addicted to alcohol when they frequently rely on it and can't remain sober for long periods.

In the UK, the new advice suggests that men and women who drink regularly should not consume more than 14 units a week, which is the equivalent of seven glasses of wine or six pints of beer.

What are the symptoms of alcohol addiction?

Like any addiction, this problem can slowly get worse, so it's important to spot the signs early. Some symptoms of alcohol addiction are:

- Drinking alcohol at inappropriate times
- Changing plans to be where alcohol is and avoiding situations where there's no alcohol
- Feeling dependent on alcohol to function
- Having a high tolerance for alcohol and not experiencing hangover symptoms
- Hiding alcohol or hiding that you are drinking it
- Finding your work and social life is becoming negatively affected because of your drinking habits
- Losing friendships because of your behaviour when you're drinking
- Feeling remorseful about your drinking
- Your family or friends are complaining that you are drinking too much

Why do some people become alcoholics?

It comes down to a complex combination of genetics, culture and social standards.

Alcohol addiction is known to run in families and you may find that each generation gives the same justification for drinking. While genetics plays an important role, there is also the social influence to take into account. Across western cultures, alcohol is readily available and binge drinking is widely accepted. The act of being drunk is associated with celebrations and we use it to relax and enjoy ourselves – even if we can't remember it the next morning! You'll often notice that we all look for reasons to drink, whether to celebrate or because we are sad, we find an excuse to have a drink.

It's impossible to pinpoint one reason why people turn to excessive alcohol use, but the rewarding effects of drinking can be largely responsible. It's well known that alcohol boosts someone's mood when they are feeling down and relaxes someone when they are feeling anxious. It is for this reason that people with high stress, anxiety or depression are more vulnerable to developing alcohol addiction. It's important to note that alcohol addiction is a real disease and a person with this addiction may not be able to control themselves and stop drinking.

Can chronic alcohol use lead to other psychological conditions?

Yes, it can. While drinking can temporarily reduce anxiety, in the long term, excessive alcohol consumption can make you more anxious and feel more depressed. Many people who suffer from psychological conditions such as insomnia and paranoia are also more likely to self-medicate with alcohol in order to relieve themselves of their symptoms.

Although it is rare, excessive alcohol consumption can cause alcohol-induced psychotic disorder (AIPD), which manifests as hallucinations, delusions and paranoia.

What are the first steps in treating alcohol addiction?

The first step in overcoming alcohol addiction is to accept that it's a problem. It's similar to any other kind of addiction or psychiatric problem and is nothing to be ashamed of. The problem is very common and seeking specialist help is very important for your mental and physical health.

As a psychiatrist, the first thing I would do is assess how much you are drinking and if there's anything in particular that triggers this habit. I would then look at your physical health, take blood tests and check if you are lacking vital vitamins. In patients who consume large amounts of alcohol, there is a risk of them developing Wernicke-Korsakoff syndrome (WKS) which is a certain type of brain disorder caused by a lack of vitamin B6. Patients who have developed this condition present a variety of issues related to memory loss and hallucinations. Treatment of this usually involves replenishing the lack of vitamin B6 and reducing alcohol intake. Then depending on the patient's situation, I might send them off to see an addiction counsellor if I believe they would benefit from this.

Detoxing from alcohol is the next step in the rehabilitation process. A lot of patients worry about the effects of an alcohol detox as the withdrawal symptoms can be quite difficult and, if not managed correctly, quite dangerous. You shouldn't be worried about going through an alcohol detox though; the correct care from a medical specialist will guide you through the withdrawal symptoms so you can focus on your recovery.

Individuals who have been drinking heavily for years are more likely to suffer more serious alcohol detox withdrawal symptoms, such as insomnia, delirium, tremors and hallucinations, than those who have recently developed the addiction. These patients are more likely to suffer minor symptoms such as nausea, headaches and anxiety.

Support from family and friends is always helpful, but there are many cases when it is an issue. Alcoholism is known to cause distress to family members, and if this is the case, then it might be a good idea to seek support from your partners or friends – you can even bring them to the appointment if you feel it would help. Encouragement throughout the process of stopping drinking is extremely helpful in your road to recovery.

Which specialist would you see for this?

Seeing your GP is usually a good start, however, some people prefer to go directly to a psychiatrist. There are also many support services around to help such as the AA; you might want to consider a rehabilitation clinic or an alcohol counsellor. More so than anything else, it's important you see someone and seek help.

7 January 2020

Causes of alcoholism

Learn more about the causes of alcoholism to begin the rehab process. Understanding the causes of alcoholism can take time but it is important in order to start the healing process.

By Boris MacKey

Alcohol Use Disorder (or AUD) is a disease where an individual becomes dependent on alcohol consumption.

It is a disease that does not have one specific cause and is diagnosed based on an evaluation of a person's behaviour and habits associated with alcohol.

There have been many studies over the years that have sought to determine what brings about this particular dependency.

And these studies have shown that alcoholism is a result of various risk factors, which we will go over in the following text.

Biological risk factors

The first 'category' of risk factors we will go over is the 'biological' category. Studies show that an individual's genetics and physiology can often play a huge role in whether or not they could develop AUD.

1. Family history

If your family has a significant history of alcoholism spanning through generations, then you have a higher risk of developing AUD.

Basically, if close family members such as your parents, grandparents, and so on, suffered from Alcohol Use Disorder, then you likely have some genes from them that make it more likely that you'll develop an alcohol problem as well.

That being said, there is not one specific gene that increases the risk. Studies have found that, in various chromosome regions, there are up to 51 various genes that could lead to Alcohol Use Disorder.

2. Through genetics or just the individual's brain alone, chemical factors can lead to AUD

When a behaviour or action evokes a pleasurable chemical response, then the brain naturally wants to repeat that behaviour or action.

And for many, alcohol consumption evokes a pleasurable chemical response. When done in moderation, this is not a bad thing.

However, those who are genetically predisposed to developing AUD, or those who simply have a tendency to overdo things, are more likely to give in to the urge to drink in an excessive manner.

They experience a positive feeling from drinking, and their brain wants more and more of it.

Eventually, their brain will become dependent on alcohol to create those 'happy chemicals', which will then lead to terrible withdrawal symptoms if the person does not drink.

Social and environmental risk factors

Along with the aforementioned genetic factors, a person could be driven to developing AUD based on the people they associate with and the environment that surrounds them.

Peer pressure: Peer pressure commonly affects teenagers and young adults. However, it can affect anybody at any age, and can often be what pushes people into what becomes an addiction. For instance, if you're attending a party or social gathering where people are drinking, then you will likely have an urge to join in. This results in the pleasurable chemical reaction, and, along with the aforementioned biological factors, could lead to you getting hooked on the habit.

Family history can apply as a social/environmental factor as well: If you grew up in a home where a parent, sibling, or other family members in the household had an alcohol problem, then you have a higher chance of developing that problem yourself. Not just due to genetics, but due to the environmental influence of growing up around alcohol abuse. Perhaps the experience caused you trauma, depression, anxiety, or other mental health issues that might tempt you to turn to alcohol as a way to cope. Or perhaps, in a way, alcohol consumption (even excessive consumption) was normalised for you. In any case, a person's family has a big impact on their risk factors for Alcohol Use Disorder, based on both biological factors and social/environmental factors.

Peer pressure from the media through advertisements, television shows, etc: There is no doubt that we are almost constantly bombarded with advertising. And advertising for alcoholic beverages is no exception. These ads often give off the impression that drinking is a fun, relaxing, harmless activity. This portrayal could have an effect on our subconscious that encourages us to drink in order to obtain those promised feelings of relaxation and happiness. And this could especially urge us to drink if we are dealing with a stressful situation. Along with these advertisements, different forms of media often portray drinking alcohol as a normal way of coping with stress. And alcoholism will often be portrayed in a lighthearted, comedic manner, which could cause some people to subconsciously downplay the severity of its real-life counterpart. Essentially, alcohol is often portrayed as something that is not dangerous. Something that will help you relax and unwind. And if someone has a desire to de-stress, chances are they will end up turning to alcohol as a result of those portrayals giving them a subliminal message that they will not develop an addiction.

Psychological factors

These factors are often the leading cause of AUD and are frequently the result of aforementioned issues such

as a family history of alcoholism or living in a negative environment.

1. Suffering from mental health

Mental health issues often lead to unhealthy coping mechanisms. And one of the most common, unfortunately, is substance abuse, particularly alcoholism.

As mentioned in a previous section, alcohol often causes a pleasurable chemical reaction which your brain will want to repeat. And if you suffer from a mental health issue such as depression, anxiety, or PTSD, then the urge might be even stronger.

People who deal with mental health disorder often seek alcohol for comfort for various reasons. Perhaps they want to gain positive feelings that they believe nothing else will bring about.

Perhaps they want to numb any psychological torment. Or perhaps it is a mix of both. In any case, mental health issues are a key factor in what brings about alcohol abuse.

2. Even if someone is dealing with 'normal' stress, they could still seek out alcohol as a coping method

Perhaps you are dealing with stress from a particular set of circumstances rather than an underlying mental health issue.

Maybe something like a significant relationship problem, an overwhelming/frustrating workplace, or an issue within your family is causing you a great deal of stress.

In any case, you might feel tempted to turn to alcohol to try and relieve those stressful feelings.

Factors leading to relapse

Even after going through rehab and being sober for a while, a person who was once addicted is almost always at risk of a relapse.

Staying sober is a lifelong challenge, but it is worthwhile. Keep in mind that, even if you have a relapse, you have not failed on your journey.

Stumbling does not mean that you should give up and fall into old habits. Keep pushing forward, and try to avoid certain factors that could lead to a severe relapse.

1. Being around another drinker

Maybe you used to go drinking with a group of people who encouraged you to do so. Or perhaps you have met some new people while being sober who drink frequently.

In either case, those people could urge you to drink, intentionally or otherwise.

It would be best to have little to no in-person interaction with the people who could encourage you to drink again. Sometimes, we have to cut people off in our lives who are negative influences.

These people are a negative influence that could cause you to fall back into an old lifestyle.

If you know some new people who drink recreationally, it would be best to simply not be around them when they're going to be drinking.

If you politely inform them of your situation, they will likely be understanding and not drink around you.

2. Highly stressful situations might tempt you to drink again

It is possible to avoid unnecessary stress. However, oftentimes, we cannot control whether or not a stressful circumstance occurs in our lives.

If you used to use alcohol to cope, then chances are you might feel a temptation to drink again once you become stressed. Remember that alcohol will only cause you more stress in the long run.

Turn to friends, family, and anyone else in your support system when you are dealing with stress, and remember healthy coping mechanisms that you have learned along the way.

Conclusion

There is no singular factor that leads to alcoholism. There are a plethora of risk factors that make it more likely for someone to develop an addiction.

If you are at high risk, it would be best to avoid drinking altogether. And if you are a recovering alcoholic, there are various factors that could trigger a relapse.

Remember to stay strong, turn to your support system, and place your focus on healthy coping mechanisms.

www.rehab4addiction.co.uk

Are you a functioning alcoholic? Know the signs

The stereotypical image of an alcoholic isn't the case for many.

By Rachel Hosie

We all know that as a society, we drink a lot. There's always a reason to drink and there are always people encouraging you to do so. When many of us think of an alcoholic, we envisage someone waking up and swigging a bottle of vodka. But this isn't always the case.

If you only drink at social occasions but you drink until you're blackout drunk each time, are you an alcoholic? What about if you drink five or six nights a week, but just a glass or two of wine per evening?

The NHS says alcohol misuse is when you drink in any way that's harmful, or when you're dependent on alcohol. To keep health risks from alcohol to a low level, both men and women are advised not to regularly drink more than 14 units a week.

According to Dr Iqbal Mohiuddi, one of the consultant psychiatrists at 25 Harley Street Day Clinic, the number of functioning alcoholics is on the rise.

There are certain signs of functioning alcoholism to look out for. Experts use the acronym CAGE.

C – Cutting down - have you ever thought you should probably drink less?

A – Annoyance - do you ever get annoyed by people nagging you about your drinking?

G – Guilt - do you ever feel guilty about your drinking or what you do as a result?

E – Eye-opener - do you ever feel like you need a drink to feel better, especially in the morning to relax?

According to Dr Mohioddi, answering yes to just a couple of the above could suggest you have a problem with alcohol.

Of course, every person is different, these are just subtle signs and answering yes doesn't necessarily make you an alcoholic, but it could be something to think about.

The NHS has a similar set of categories to consider whether you might be misusing alcohol: you feel you should cut down on your drinking, other people have been criticising your drinking, you feel guilty or bad about your drinking or you need a drink first thing in the morning to steady your nerves or get rid of a hangover.

It says: 'Someone you know may be misusing alcohol if: they regularly drink more than 14 units of alcohol a week, they're sometimes unable to remember what happened the night before, and they fail to do what was expected of them as a result of their drinking (for example, missing an appointment or work because they're drunk or hungover).'

Dr Mohiuddi estimates that a third to a half of the clients he treats for alcohol addiction don't fit the stereotypical image we hold of an addict.

'They're working in high-powered jobs, in the City or the media and drinking heavily is accepted, almost expected,' he told Healthista.

'They have carried on for years in this way but suddenly they're getting physical symptoms such as feeling sick in the mornings and needing a drink and perhaps a partner has said they have had enough and it's the drink or them.

'Conversely, as more companies become aware of drinking issues in the workplace, they may send people in for detox treatment to protect the health of their valued employee.'

Dr Mohioddi says functioning alcoholics can usually keep on top of all their responsibilities despite their drinking, and are usually in denial about their alcohol intake.

Many people think they're OK because they have a few alcohol-free days of the week, but they then binge at the weekend, causing serious damage.

And it's likely that you're binge-drinking more than you realise - anything more than four units (one being a small glass of wine, half a pint of beer or a 1.5 ounce shot of a spirit) is classified as a binge.

'During a binge your body is literally saturated with alcohol and even though you think you can tolerate it, your body isn't breaking it down any quicker,' Dr Mohioddi says.

'A good mantra to keep in mind is that human beings can only tolerate one unit of alcohol in an hour so try and stick to that.'

If you are worried about your drinking or even just curious, you can take the Alcohol Change drinking quiz to see if it's likely to be affecting your health.

You'll be asked a few simple questions about your drinking habits, like how often you drink and how many units you consume in an average week.

Alcoholics Anonymous helpline is open 24/7 on 0800 9177 650. If you would prefer, you can also email them at help@aamail.org or live chat via their website at www.alcoholics-anonymous.org.uk.

Drinkline, a free, confidential helpline for people who are concerned about their drinking, or someone else's. Call 0300 123 1110 (weekdays 9am–8pm, weekends 11am–4pm)

18 September 2020

'The day I started drinking vodka in the morning, I realised I had a serious problem'

I had always been an enthusiastic drinker, but during lockdown I became progressively more dependent on it, until I reached crisis point.

By Charlotte Southall

Just over a year ago, on May 25, 2020, I found myself pouring a glass of vodka at 10.30 am. It was a line I never imagined I would cross. Drinking was something to do at night, I thought, in the sweaty heat of a pub or bar, or on your living room sofa, in front of the television after a long day of work.

But just an hour or so after waking up, there I was, in my kitchen, sipping vodka from a glass. The taste felt immediately wrong I realised I had a serious problem.

It came as no surprise to read the warning last month from doctors that lockdown might have created a dark legacy of alcohol abuse in the UK. Just as the cancellation of routine medical appointments has created a worrying backlog in cancer diagnoses, experts worry that successive lockdowns might have created a new generation of dependent drinkers still mostly hidden from the NHS's view. These 'Covid drinkers' seem to be concentrated among the middle-aged, including many in stressful high-level jobs.

I was an enthusiastic drinker ever since I was 18 (I'm now 33). During my 20s, life revolved around the weekend. In the middle of the week, I'd buy a new outfit, excitedly planning a night out with my girlfriends. Then, we'd hit the pubs and bars near my home in Lytham, Lancashire. I would usually end up drunker than my friends; I always woke up the next morning with a terrible hangover.

Work was never an issue. I'm employed with my family's energy business, and my parents were always hugely tolerant. If one day I couldn't get up to work on time, it was usually overlooked.

But then came Covid, and my drinking habits began to seep ever more into the week. With no opportunity to see friends, I turned more and more to the comfort of the bottle. With gyms shut, my exercise routine collapsed.

The weather was beautiful last April; it started to feel like I was living on holiday. Each afternoon, I finished work and opened a bottle of Prosecco in the garden with my partner. Soon, I was drinking two or three bottles of wine each evening. Other nights, I made vodka mojitos, thinking I would drink less. But whatever I drank, I drank to excess.

As April turned into May, I began to pass out on my garden chair each evening. My mental health deteriorated rapidly. I woke each morning with the most horrendous anxiety I'd ever experienced. Paralysing, debilitating dread, spreading across my body.

I treated it the only way I knew how: with more alcohol. Usually, I was able to hold off until the afternoon – then, as soon as it felt vaguely acceptable, I treated myself to a drink to calm my nerves. It always worked – temporarily, at least. I was living by the hair of the dog mantra – the popular but dangerous idea that the way to get rid of a hangover is by drinking more.

My boyfriend, understandably, was not happy. At first, he used to join me for a drink in the garden, but then he would stop after a healthy amount, while I carried on, drinking myself into oblivion. Some days he would come home from a day's work to find me unconscious in the garden. I would lie incessantly, telling him I'd had only one drink. I began to buy more than I needed to so I could hide some away from his sight, in case I needed a tipple in the middle of the night. He would find booze stashed under the bed; it felt like a cruel betrayal.

I wasn't much fun to be around in that sorry state. At a few points, he decided to leave for a few days to stay with his mother.

Then came that landmark May bank holiday weekend. On Sunday evening, I invited some friends over to my garden for Prosecco. As usual, I drank until I was unconscious. I woke on Monday morning in a state of total dread and found my hand reaching for the vodka bottle. I felt stuck: I didn't have the strength to get through the day without a drink but knew that having the drink would turn the day into a disaster.

My partner came home from walking our dog to find me a distraught mess. I told him: 'I can't do this any more; I wish you'd just give me some tablets that would send me to sleep so I don't have to go through this.'

I sobbed to my mother down the phone. I knew if I didn't sort this out I would turn into a stereotypical alcoholic. She managed to secure me a place on a six-week residential rehabilitation programme at Delamere Health in Cheshire. That evening, I drank a few final glasses of wine; I knew it would be the last alcohol of my life. The next morning, Mum picked me up and drove me to the rehab centre.

The first few days were a whirlwind. I met others in my position and was assigned a counsellor. I began to learn so much about how my drinking was shaping my life in ways I hadn't even understood. I felt like I'd gone to university, and studied a degree on my behaviour and personality.

I realised that I'd looked at life for the past six years through a negative, critical lens. If friends had to cancel plans, I assumed it was because they didn't like me. I'd take their rejection to heart and send them an unfriendly message. It was all because of my alcoholic brain, I realised.

I learnt just how destructive my behaviour had been: all those nights out when my friends had travelled home at a reasonable time, whereas I would end up back at the house of somebody I barely knew, drinking until the early hours. Even a family meal could end this way.

I've been dry ever since getting out. My mind feels clearer, and my life feels under control. My relationship with my boyfriend is strong.

Before I got sober I used to think I drank to gain confidence; now, I'm dry, I seem to have confidence I've never had before. I can go out and enjoy myself, feeling comfortable in my skin, without a drop of booze.

It's difficult sometimes, of course. I can't help feeling like a black sheep at a friend's birthday, as the only one not drinking. But I know deep in my brain that if I have just one sip, I won't be able to stop.

My life is on the mend. In a strange way, I'll always be grateful to that bank holiday weekend, when I crossed the Rubicon with my first drink of the morning. It raised the alarm bell, forcing me onto the right path. I'm not going back.

As told to Luke Mintz

4 June 2021

What is drink spiking? How can you know if it's happened to you, and how can it be prevented?

An article from *The Conversation*.

THE CONVERSATION

By Nicole Lee, Professor at the National Drug Research Institute (Melbourne), Curtin University & Jarryd Bartle, Sessional Lecturer, RMIT University

Recent media reports suggest drink spiking at pubs and clubs may be on the rise.

'Drink spiking' is when someone puts alcohol or other drugs into another person's drink without their knowledge.

It can include:

- putting alcohol into a non-alcoholic drink
- adding extra alcohol to an alcoholic drink
- slipping prescription or illegal drugs into an alcoholic or non-alcoholic drink.

Alcohol is actually the drug most commonly used in drink spiking.

The use of other drugs, such as benzodiazepines (like Rohypnol), GHB or ketamine is relatively rare.

These drugs are colourless and odourless so they are less easily detected. They cause drowsiness, and can cause 'blackouts' and memory loss at high doses.

Perpetrators may spike victims' drinks to commit sexual assault. But according to the data, the most common type of drink spiking is to 'prank' someone or some other non-criminal motive.

So how can you know if your drink has been spiked, and as a society, how can we prevent it?

How often does it happen?

We don't have very good data on how often drink spiking occurs. It's often not reported to police because victims can't remember what has happened.

If a perpetrator sexually assaults someone after spiking their drink, there are many complex reasons why victims may not want to report to police.

One study, published in 2004, estimated there were about 3,000 to 4,000 suspected drink spiking incidents a year in Australia. It estimated less than 15% of incidents were reported to police.

It found four out of five victims were women. About half were under 24 years old and around one-third aged 25-34. Two-thirds of the suspected incidents occurred in licensed venues like pubs and clubs.

According to an Australian study from 2006, around 3% of adult sexual assault cases occurred after perpetrators intentionally drugged victims outside of their knowledge.

It's crucial to note that sexual assault is a moral and legal violation, whether or not the victim was intoxicated and whether or not the victim became intoxicated voluntarily.

How can you know if it's happened to you?

Some of the warning signs your drink might have been spiked include:

- feeling light-headed, or like you might faint
- feeling quite sick or very tired
- feeling drunk despite only having a very small amount of alcohol
- passing out
- feeling uncomfortable and confused when you wake up, with blanks in your memory about what happened the previous night.

If you think your drink has been spiked, you should ask someone you trust to get you to a safe place, or talk to venue staff or security if you're at a licensed venue. If you feel very unwell you should seek medical attention.

If you believe your drink has been spiked or you have been sexually assaulted, contact the police to report the incident.

How can drink spiking be prevented?

Most drink spiking occurs at licensed venues like pubs and clubs. Licensees and people who serve alcohol have a responsibility to provide a safe environment for patrons, and have an important role to play in preventing drink spiking.

This includes having clear procedures in place to ensure staff understand the signs of drink spiking, including with alcohol.

Preventing drink spiking is a collective responsibility, not something to be shouldered by potential victims.

Licensees can take responsible steps including:

- removing unattended glasses
- reporting suspicious behaviour
- declining customer requests to add extra alcohol to a person's drink
- supplying water taps instead of large water jugs
- promoting responsible consumption of alcohol, including discouraging rapid drinking
- being aware of 'red flag' drink requests, such as repeated shots, or double or triple shots, or adding vodka to beer or wine.

A few simple precautions everyone can take to reduce the risk of drink spiking include:

- have your drink close to you, keep an eye on it and don't leave it unattended
- avoid sharing beverages with other people
- purchase or pour your drinks yourself
- if you're offered a drink by someone you don't know well, go to the bar with them and watch the bartender pour your drink
- if you think your drink tastes weird, pour it out
- keep an eye on your friends and their beverages too.

20 May 2021

Drink driving

The risks, the law, the limits and the penalties.

Drink-driving is one of the biggest killers on our roads with even small amounts of alcohol impairing driving and increasing risk.

In this fact page we will cover:

- the effects of alcohol on driving
- the drink-driving laws in the UK
- the penalties for drink-driving in the UK
- how to assess your fitness to drive

How alcohol affects your driving

Alcohol is a depressant and even small amounts (such as half a pint of lager) affect reaction times, judgement and co-ordination. Alcohol also makes you drowsy and affects vision and how you judge speed and distance.

Drivers who drink-drive are also not able to assess their own impairment because alcohol creates a false sense of confidence. This means that drivers are more inclined to take risks and believe they are in control when they are not. For these reasons, the only way for drivers to be safe is to not drink anything at all before driving: feeling sober is not a reliable indication that you are safe to drive.

' If you're driving, it's better to have none for the road '

Statement from the Government's Think! campaign

The law and the limits of drink-driving in the UK

In England and Wales, it's legal to drive with a blood-alcohol concentration (BAC) of 80 milligrams of alcohol per 100 millilitres of blood (80mg/100ml). This is the highest limit in Europe.

In most of Europe, including Scotland, the blood alcohol limit is 50mg/100ml, and in many countries it is even lower. For example, in Sweden, the legal limit is 20mg/100ml for all drivers – effectively zero tolerance – while Hungary, Romania, Slovakia and the Czech Republic do not allow drivers to drink any alcohol at all.

There is no failsafe way to tell how much alcohol will put you over the limit, or to convert the BAC limit into how many units you can have: the concentration of alcohol in blood depends on various factors. These include your weight, age, gender, or how much you have eaten before drinking. That's why the only safe amount to drink if you're driving is nothing at all – not a drop.

The penalties for drink-driving in the UK

In the UK if a driver is found to be over the drink-drive limit, and/or driving while impaired by alcohol, they can receive a maximum penalty of six months in prison, an unlimited fine and an automatic driving ban of at least one year.

Drink-drive rehabilitation courses

Drivers who have been found guilty of drink-driving and who have been banned for 12 months or more may be

In the UK, more than 200 people die every year, in a drink-drive related crash

6x
more likely to be involved in a fatal crash, if you have 50-80 mg alcohol per 100ml blood, compared to 0ml

3x
more likely to die on the roads, if you have 20-50mg alcohol per 100ml of blood, compared to 0ml

46%
more likely to be at fault in road collisions, if you have 10mg alcohol per 100ml, compared to 0ml

England & Wales have the highest drink-drive limit in Europe: 80mg alcohol per 100ml of blood

Random drink and drug testing is supported by 72% of UK drivers (Brake report, 2019)

offered the chance to take a rehabilitation course to reduce their driving ban.

High-risk offenders

High-risk offenders are drivers who:

- were convicted of 2 drink driving offences within 10 years
- were driving with an alcohol reading of at least 87.5 microgrammes of alcohol per 100ml of breath, 200mg of alcohol per 100ml of blood, or 267.5mg of alcohol per 100ml of urine
- refused to give the police a sample of breath, blood or urine to test for alcohol
- refused to allow a sample of blood to be tested for alcohol

These offenders need to pass a medical examination with a DVLA appointed doctor to prove their fitness to drive, prior to receiving a new licence.

Causing death while under the influence of alcohol

If a driver kills someone while under the influence of alcohol, they can be charged with causing death by careless driving while under the influence of drink or drugs (Section 3A of the Road Traffic Act 1988 (as amended by the Road Traffic Act 1991, section 3)), which carries a maximum penalty of 14 years in prison and an unlimited fine.

How the police catch drink-driving

In the UK, the police can stop and breathalyse you if they have reason to suspect you have been drinking – for example, if you are driving erratically. They can also breathalyse you if you have committed another traffic offence (such as speeding or driving without a seat belt) or if you are involved in a crash.

In many countries, the police have the power to stop and breathalyse drivers at random, with no need to suspect the driver is under the influence. For example, police may randomly test drivers near pubs and clubs late at night. Random testing is allowed in most EU countries and has been found to be highly effective in reducing drink-drive casualties without over-burdening the police and criminal justice system. At present, random testing is not permitted in the UK.

How to assess your fitness to drive

To be safe, drivers should ensure they are completely sober before driving – including the following day.

There's no way of knowing exactly how long it takes to sober up completely after drinking, but it's longer than many people think. As a rough guide, drivers should allow at least one hour to absorb alcohol, plus at least one hour for each unit consumed – but it can take longer, so it's wise to leave extra time to be safe.

For example, if you finish drinking three pints of strong lager or one bottle of 12% ABV wine (both nine units) at midnight, you will not be rid of alcohol until at least 9am. If you have a heavy and/or late night drinking you could be impaired all of the next day. Drinking coffee, eating, sleeping and showering don't make you sober up any faster. It just takes time.

Factors influencing the effect of alcohol

How long it takes for alcohol to leave your system varies depending on lots of factors, including:

- Gender – men tend to process alcohol faster than women;
- Dehydration – if you haven't drunk enough fluids, alcohol will stay in your system for longer;
- Mixers – mixing drinks with water and juice means you absorb alcohol slower, fizzy mixers mean you absorb alcohol faster than with no mixers;
- Tiredness – when you're tired your liver becomes less efficient, processing alcohol more slowly so it stays in your system for longer.

Brake advises people who need to drive the next day to limit themselves to one or two drinks.

How much alcohol is in your drink

The alcohol content of drinks is measured in units. A UK unit is eight grams (or 10 millilitres) of pure alcohol. Below is a list of some popular drinks and how many units they contain:

- A single shot (25ml measure) of 40% spirit (e.g. gin, whisky or vodka): one unit
- A pint of 4.5% beer: 2.3 units
- A large (250ml) glass of 13% wine: 3.2 units
- A pint of 6% cider: 3.4 units

It's simple, if you're going to drive, don't drink and if you've had a drink, never drive. Any amount of alcohol impairs your driving.

Alcohol and your mood

Although we don't always think of it as such, alcohol is a psychoactive substance, meaning it can radically change the way we think and feel. Here, we look at some of the ways that alcohol can change our mood and our behaviour, and how it does that.

"Alcohol has been described as a 'favourite coping mechanism' in the UK."

The feel-good factor

The human brain uses a number of chemicals – known as neurotransmitters – to carry messages. One of the most important of these is dopamine, which is often thought of as a 'happy hormone'. When we start drinking alcohol, our bodies produce extra dopamine, which travels to the parts of the brain known as 'reward centres' – the bits that make us feel good and make us want to do more of whatever we're doing.

So, our first couple of drinks are likely to make us feel good. They're also likely to make us want more to drink. However, if we continue drinking, the dopamine high will eventually be pushed aside by the less pleasant effects of alcohol: confusion, clumsiness, nausea and dehydration.

Loss of inhibitions

Alcohol is sometimes described as a 'disinhibitor' – it makes us less cautious and more inclined to do things we would normally be shy or hesitant about. Sometimes, we might be quite glad of that. Sometimes it can lead us to do things that may be a bit annoying but not particularly problematic, like singing loudly or talking too much. Other times, the consequences can be more serious – for example if we say something hurtful we regret later on, or try to drive ourselves home.

Alcohol is also a depressant and slows down the parts of the brain where we make decisions and consider consequences, making us less likely to think about what might happen if we do something.

Depression

Although alcohol is often described as a 'depressant', that's not quite the same as saying it will make you depressed. In small doses, alcohol can make you feel quite cheerful for a short while. What alcohol does, though, is depress the body's central nervous system – the system that lets our brain tell our body what to do. That means that alcohol makes us less co-ordinated, more accident-prone, and less aware of danger.

However, alcohol can make us feel depressed too. The hangover after a heavy drinking session can be a thoroughly miserable experience. A combination of dehydration, low blood sugar, and various by-products of alcohol can leave us struggling to move or think.

In the longer-term, the body becomes used to the dopamine boosts it's getting from alcohol, and starts making less dopamine to compensate. That means that if drinking becomes a habit, we may become dopamine-deficient and this could contribute to us experiencing low mood.

Anxiety

Alcohol has been described as a 'favourite coping mechanism' in the UK and is commonly used to try and manage stress and anxiety, particularly in social situations, giving us what's sometimes called 'Dutch courage'. Since alcohol can increase the body's production of dopamine and serotonin, two of the body's 'happy hormones', it can temporarily make us feel less anxious.

Long term drinking, however, can lower levels of both these hormones as well as lowering blood sugar and increasing dehydration, leading to worse anxiety. There is also a risk of becoming reliant on alcohol to manage anxiety, leading to other physical and mental health problems.

What to do if you're struggling

If you are feeling anxious, low or experiencing any other symptoms of mental health problems, or you think that you are drinking too much, you deserve support. You can speak to your GP, and get advice and help at www.mind.org.uk and www.alcoholchange.org.uk

Mum of teenager who died after drinking alcohol sends warning

By Georgia Banks

New figures for teenage alcohol consumption suggest that nine in ten North-East children aged 15 or younger are not drinking regularly – but worryingly one in three who drink are drinking more since the start of the pandemic.

Alcohol services and a grieving mum whose daughter died after drinking alcohol aged 16 have responded with alarm to results from the survey by Balance, which also show that strong spirits like vodka are frequently consumed.

The findings give pause for thought to parents thinking about supplying alcohol for teenage children this summer.

And after a year in which the pandemic has disrupted the lives of many teenagers, teachers have backed chief medical officer guidance for parents to help children avoid alcohol as long as possible at a crucial time in their education.

North Tyneside mum Joanne Good tragically lost her 16-year-old daughter Megan when she didn't wake up on New Year's Day 2014, after drinking alcohol at a friend's party.

Commenting on the findings of the youth survey, she said: 'Losing Megan devastated our family, and I don't ever want another parent to go through what we have been through. I think it's so important to educate people from a young age about the dangers of alcohol and share real life experiences. I've been into schools and when the pupils hear what happened to Megan, it really makes them sit up and listen.

'I'm concerned that some teenagers say they're drinking more alcohol since the pandemic. It's really worrying to see that even children under 16 are drinking at such a young age.

'As a parent, I know myself what it's like to have teenagers and they're always going to want to try things, but alcohol is so normalised these days and it's passed down through the generations. It doesn't have to be that way. Alcohol is harming our young people. I know first-hand the tragic consequences it can have. Talk to your children, tell them about Megan. Don't reinforce the "good" side of alcohol.'

2 June 2021

Alcohol and the Law – The law and underage drinking

It is important to be aware of guidelines, facts and the law about alcohol in the UK.

Under 5?

It is illegal to give alcohol to under 5s.

Under 16?

It is at the landlord's discretion as to whether children are allowed anywhere in a pub. They cannot, of course, buy or drink alcohol on the premises.

Under 18?

If you are under 18, it is illegal to buy alcohol (this includes in any shop or supermarket, off licenses, bars, clubs or restaurants and buying on line). It is illegal to buy alcohol for someone under 18 in a licensed premises, the only exception is for 16 or 17 year-olds who are allowed to drink beer, wine or cider with food if with an adult (but they may not buy the alcohol themselves).

It is legal for anyone over 5 to drink alcohol. The restrictions apply to purchasing (under 18) and location – in licensed premises, in public or in alcohol exclusion zones. Police have powers to confiscate alcohol from under 18's drinking in public spaces (e.g. in the street or in parks).

The UK Chief Medical Officers (CMO) recommend that parents should not allow their children to drink alcohol at home under the age of 15.

Children and their parents and carers are advised that an alcohol-free childhood is the healthiest and best option. However, if children drink alcohol, it should not be until at least the age of 15 years.

If young people aged 15 to 17 years consume alcohol it should always be with the guidance of a parent or carer or in a supervised environment.

Parents and young people should be aware that drinking, even at age 15 or older, can be hazardous to health and that not drinking is the healthiest option for young people.

If 15 to 17 year-olds do consume alcohol they should do so infrequently and certainly on no more than one day a week. Young people aged 15 to 17 years should never exceed recommended Government guidelines.

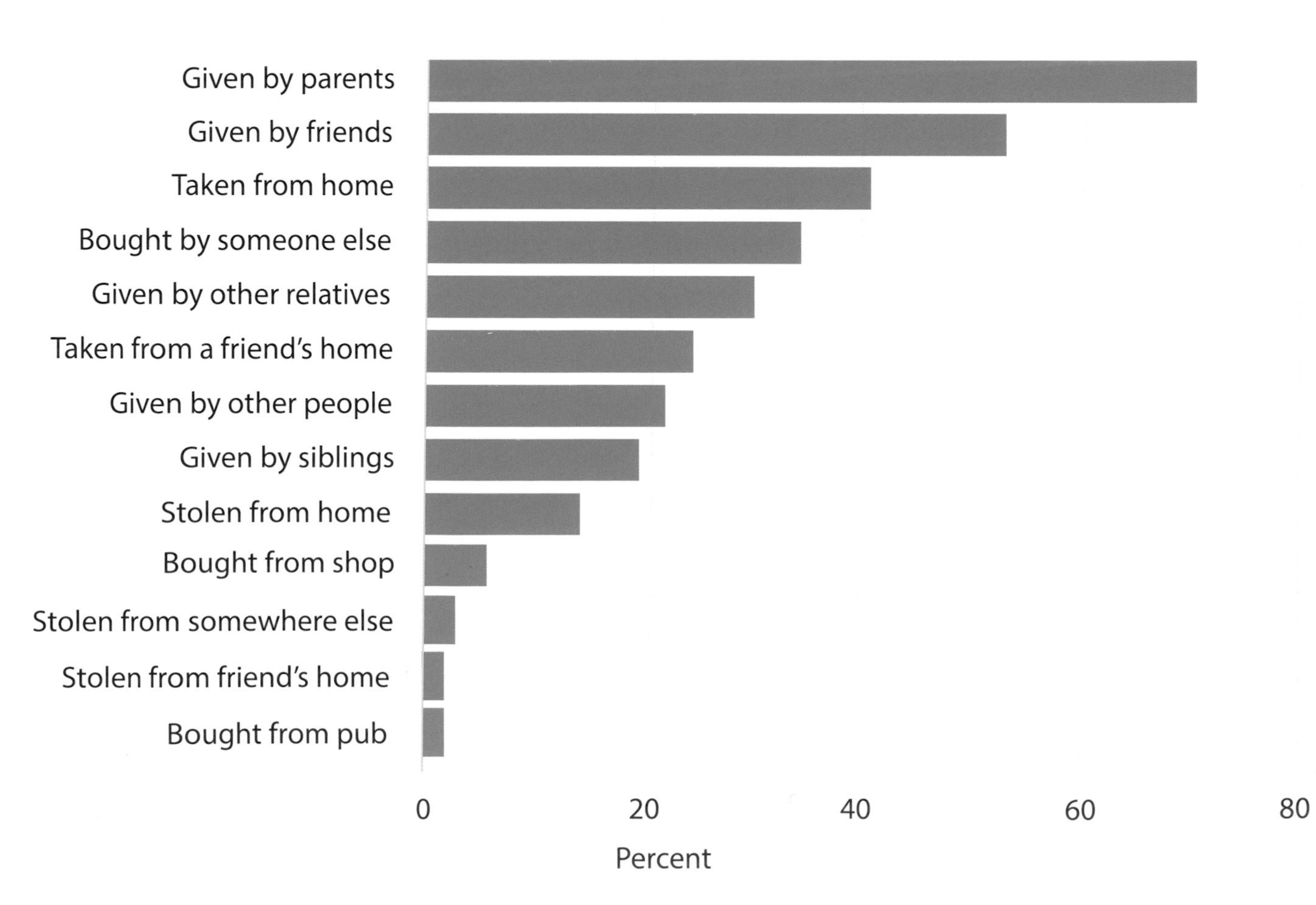

Source: NHS Digital: Statistics on Alcohol, England, 2018 'How young people aged 11-15 obtained alcohol in the last four weeks'

Can I let my kids drink at home?

Some parents allow their children to try a little alcohol with them on special occasions; others prefer not to. There is some evidence that shows drinking at an earlier age increases the possibility of alcohol-related harm later on, but other studies show young people introduced to drinking moderately in the home, with good parental role models, are less likely to binge and more likely to develop moderate drinking habits. Remember, there is a world of difference between sips on special occasions and whole drinks, so the UK Chief Medical Officers (CMO) recommend that parents should not allow their children to drink alcohol at home under the age of 15.

Whatever you decide, stick to your guns and make sure your child understands why it can be dangerous for young people to drink. Be prepared to say NO if you are uncomfortable with party situations and lay down ground rules. Children should also know that there are laws restricting the age at which you can buy and drink alcohol.

With older teenagers, you need to aim for a balance: warning them of the dangers and making them aware of the law; but also saying that they can enjoy moderate social drinking when they're adults if they choose to. The important thing is to focus on the facts, and to give your child the knowledge and skills to avoid the dangers associated with alcohol.

Drinking and driving

It's against the law to drive with more than 80mg (milligrams) alcohol per 100ml (millilitres) of blood, or 50mg in Scotland. If you break the law, you face having your licence taken away for at least a year and an unlimited fine or up to six months in prison. Causing death through drink-driving can result in a maximum prison sentence of 14 years and a driving ban for at least two years.

Buying alcohol for those under 18

Police have the power to charge those over 18 who knowingly buy alcohol for anyone under the legal drinking age (buying by proxy). It is important that older friends and family know that they could be charged for supplying alcohol irresponsibly. As it is increasingly difficult for under 18's to buy alcohol, parents are now the main providers of alcohol for this age group (70%) putting a huge responsibility on you to keep youngsters safe and out of trouble.

When do Brits start drinking?

Vast majority of UK adults say they tried booze well before age 18, with most having partaken by the age of 15.

By Connor Ibbetson, Data Journalist

Whether it's a pint in the local or a sip of wine with dinner, for many people their first alcoholic drink is a rite of passage. But at what age does this usually happen? And at what age would parents like it to happen?

YouGov RealTime asked how old Britons were when they had their first drink, and the most common answer was age 16 (given by 17% of respondents). But if we look at the cumulative total we can see that half (55%) of Brits had tried alcohol for the first time by the time they turned 15.

Only 9% say they waited until the legal drinking age and, in fact, the vast majority (81%) of adults say they had already tried alcohol by their 18th birthday. One in four (25%) Brits say they had tried alcohol well before legal age, at 13 or younger.

Men are more likely to have tried alcohol at a younger age, with one in five (22%) having tried it at age 12 or before, compared to just 14% of women.

Would Brits be willing to let their children get away with the same as they did, however? YouGov also asked Brits when they would be willing to let their children drink, and most adults say they wouldn't allow it before the age of 16 - and when it comes to spirits they want them to wait until 18.

A plurality (a group that is the largest but not a majority) of Brits say they would let their kids have wine (23%) or beer and cider (24%) starting at age 16. However, a third (36%) of Brits would be happy to let their kids have beer or cider before age 16, while 34% would also give them wine before 16.

The YouGov RealTime research also finds a notable class divide when it comes to giving children wine. Approaching two thirds (62%) of adults from an ABC1 background would be happy to give their children wine when they were 16 or younger, compared to 49% of adults from a C2DE background who say the same. This same pattern is repeated for beer

Most Brits say they tried alcohol before 18

At what age, if at all, did you have your first alcoholic drink? (%)

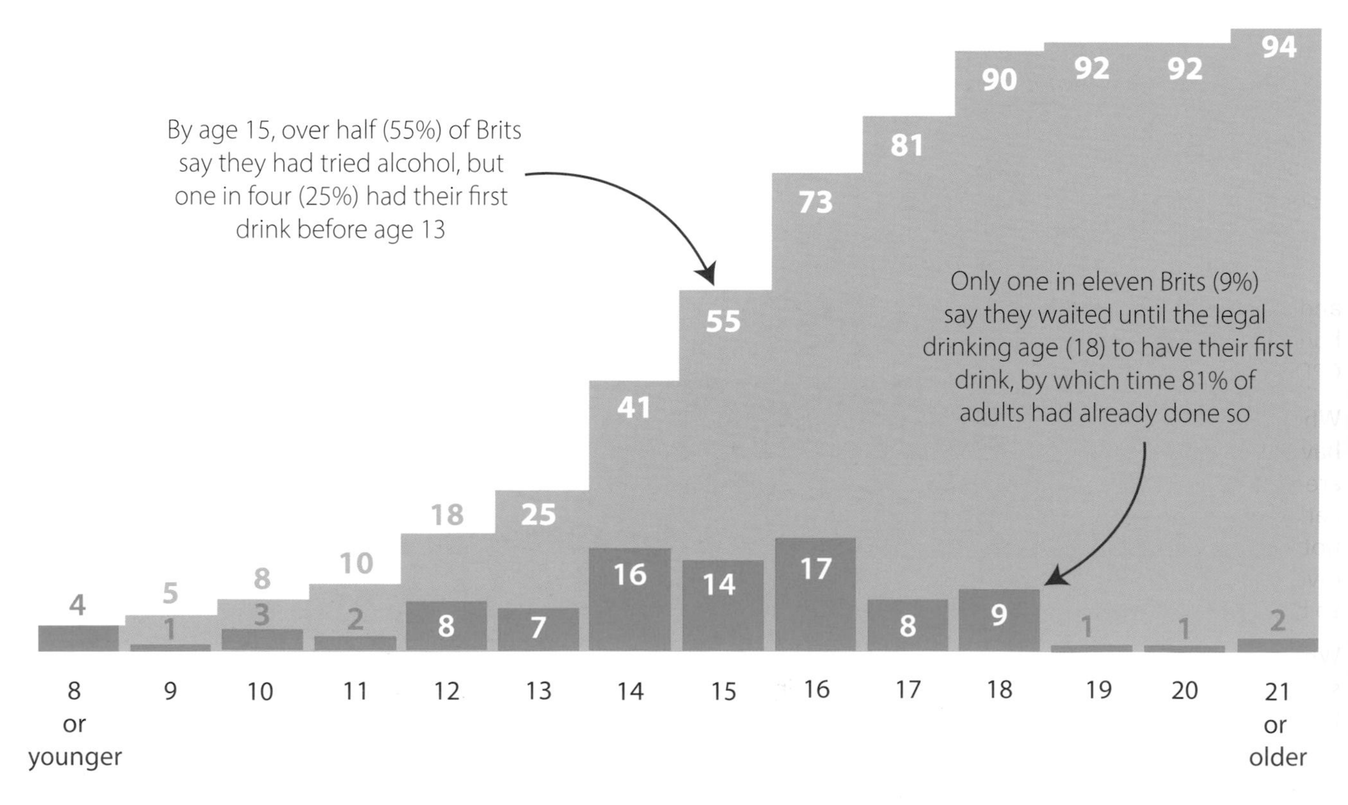

What age would Brits let their kids have various types of booze?

For the following question, even if you do not have a child(ren), please imagine that you did. At what age, if at all, would you allow your child(ren) to drink the following types pf alcoholic drinks? (%)

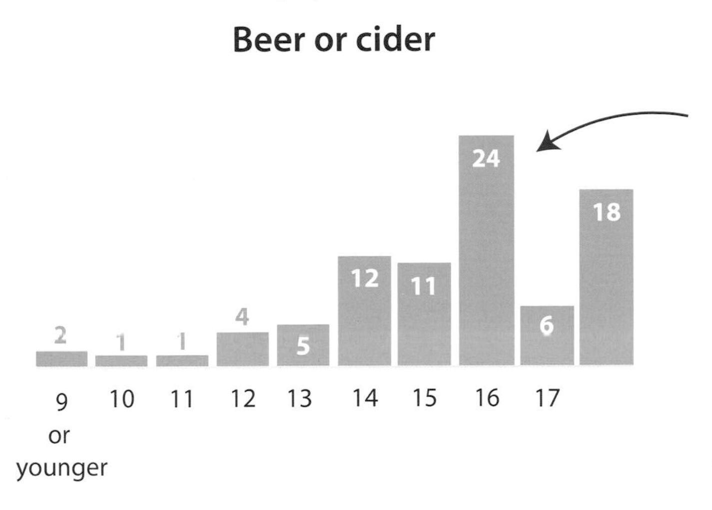

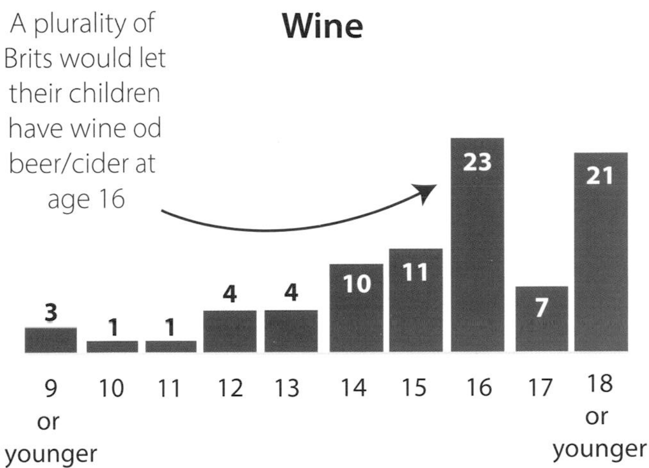

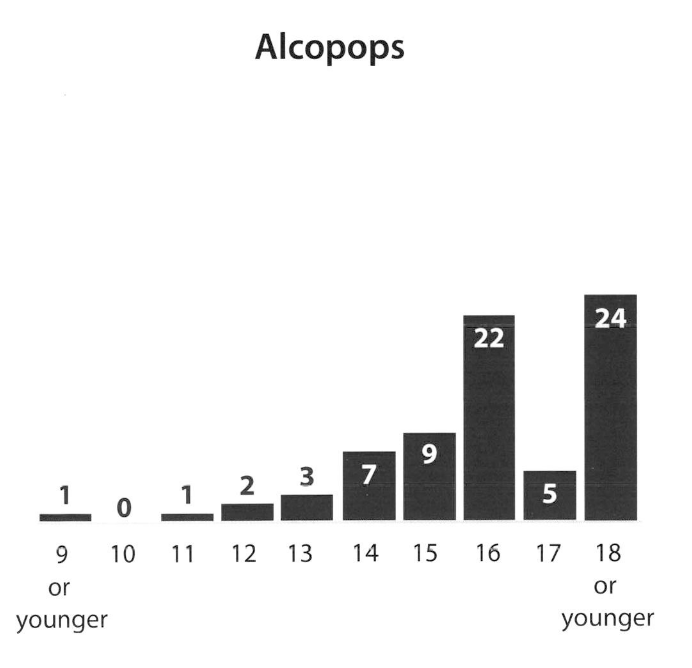

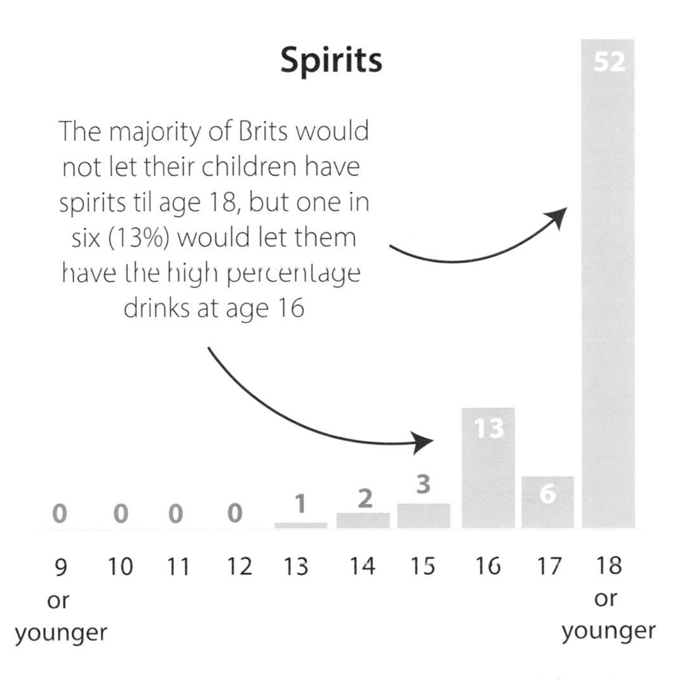

Source: YouGov 27 -28 August 2020

and cider, with 65% of ABC1 background adults happy to hand the booze over at 16 or before compared to 49% of C2DE adults.

When it comes to alcopops, despite the drinks typically having a low alcohol percentage (between 3% and 7%), Brits are slightly less willing to give them to their offspring at an early age. Nearly a quarter (24%) of adults say they would not let their kids have these until age 18. A fifth (22%) would give them to their children at age 16, with 23% happy to do so before their child turned 16.

When it comes to stronger drinks Brits are more likely to say their children will need to wait until legal drinking age. Half (52%) wouldn't give their children spirits such as vodka and whisky until they were 18, but 13% of adults would be willing to do so when their child hit 16 years of age.

Younger adults are more likely to be lenient with their children and drinking, for example 22% of 18 to 24 year olds would let their children have spirits at age 16, compared to only 9% of over 65s who say the same.

1 October 2020

Key data on young people - Alcohol

An extract.

Adolescent alcohol consumption patterns have been a concern for many years but recent trend data have been encouraging, generally showing a decline. *The International Health Behaviour of School Aged Children* study has shown, for example, that many of the European countries involved have seen a decline in alcohol use in parallel with an increase in the number of adolescents who abstain from alcohol use altogether (Inchley et al, 2018).

66%
of those aged 11-15 say they have never drunk alcohol

Source: HSCIC (2017), Smoking, Drinking and Drug Use Among Young People in England in 2016

In England, 23% of 15 year olds who drank reported having been drunk in the last four weeks in 2016

Source: HSCIC (2017), Smoking, Drinking and Drug Use Among Young People in England in 2016

In 2016 the *English Smoking, Drinking and Drug Use* survey reported that 66% of secondary school pupils aged 11-15 said they have never drunk alcohol. The majority had tried it by the time they were 15 (68%), but only 24% of 15 year olds had drunk it in the previous week (NHS Digital, 2017).

Estimates of alcohol consumption by 11-15 year olds from around the UK are also available from studies such as the HBSC study and the *Scottish Schools Adolescent Lifestyle and Substance Use Survey* (SALSUS), although the data relate to slightly different years and sometimes different questions are asked. Despite this, reports tend to be generally comparable, with low rates of regular drinking in single digits for 11 and 13 year olds, and higher rates for 15 year olds. In the SDDU study in England, rates went up from 6% for 11 year olds to 24% for 15 year olds. The 2014 HBSC Wales survey reported that 6% of 11 year olds had drunk alcohol at least once a week, compared to 14% of 15 year olds. HBSC Scotland also reported 14% of 15 year olds consumed alcohol. Also in Scotland the SALSUS study reported that 4% of 13 year olds and 17% of 15 year olds had drunk alcohol in the seven days prior to being surveyed.

Chart 4.13 shows that although rates of drinking among secondary school aged children as reported in the English SDDU are still historically very low, there appeared to be a slight rise in prevalence rates between 2014 and 2016. However, the question on alcohol consumption was changed in 2016, as it appeared there may have been some under reporting previously due to a misunderstanding around what a 'proper' or 'low alcohol' drink was (both elements included in the original question). The authors suggest that 'Whilst this means the survey now gives an improved picture of the proportion of young people who have drunk alcohol, comparisons with previous years are not possible.' (NHS Digital, 2017, p35.)

Chart 4.13 also confirms that rates of drinking increase with age. The rise in reports of drinking at age 13/14 may make Year 9 a potentially important group to target with alcohol related health promotion interventions.

Being drunk is a key indicator of alcohol misuse. The SDDU survey suggested that nearly a quarter (23%) of 15 year olds who admitted drinking reported being drunk in the last four weeks. The SDDU also reports some interesting statistics on where young people get alcohol. In terms of framing interventions, it is useful to know that 61% of current drinkers aged 11-15 said they never buy alcohol themselves. The most common sources are being given it by parents or friends, or taking it from home. Pupils who lived with

Chart 4.13: Prevalence of drinking alcohol in the last week, age 11-15, England, 2003-2016

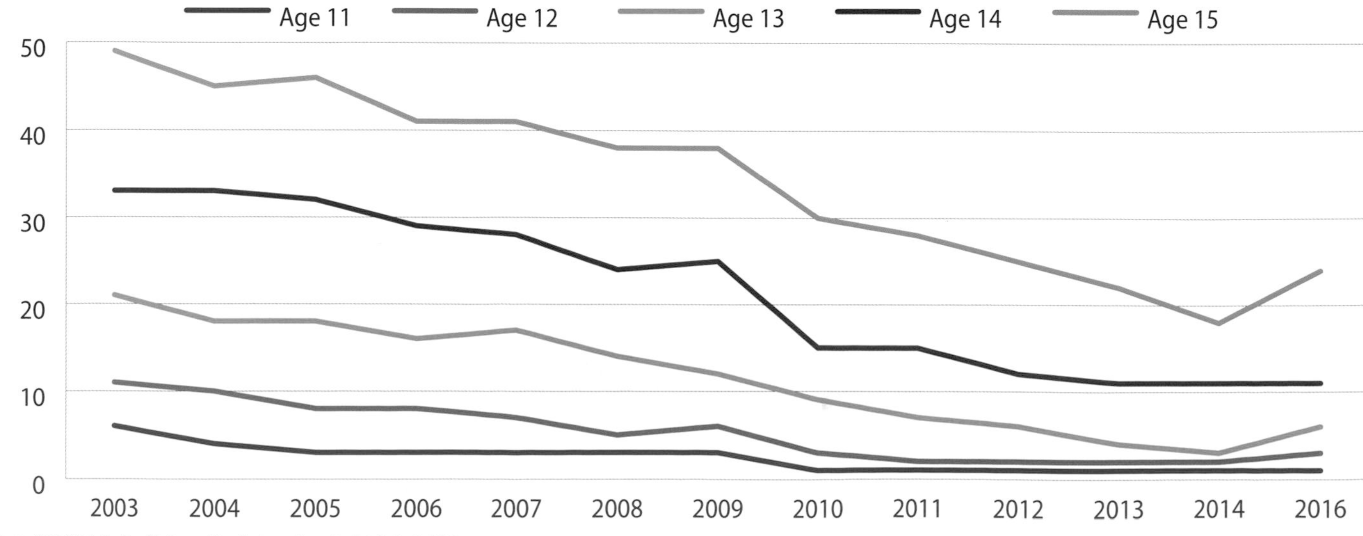

Source: HSCIC (2017), Smoking, Drinking and Drug Use Among Young People in England in 2016

Chart 4.14: Alcohol consumption (more than 14 units per week) trends in 16-24 year olds by gender, England, 2011-2017

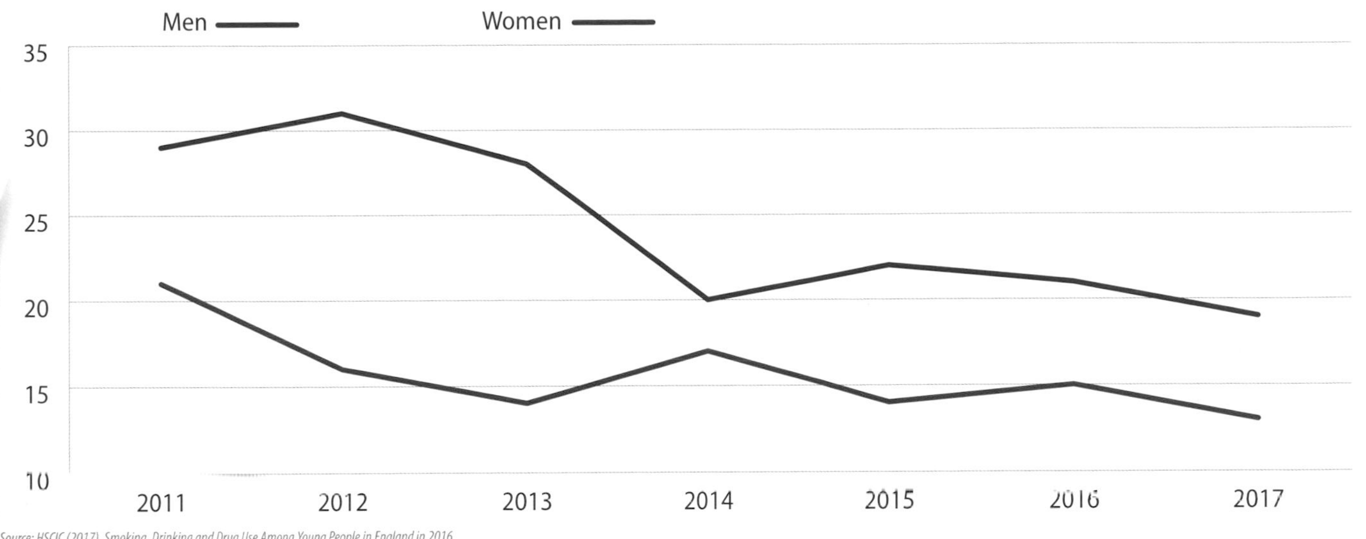

Source: HSCIC (2017), Smoking, Drinking and Drug Use Among Young People in England in 2016

Chart 4.15: Alcohol-related NHS hospital admissions by age, England, 2017/18, including primary and secondary cause of admission

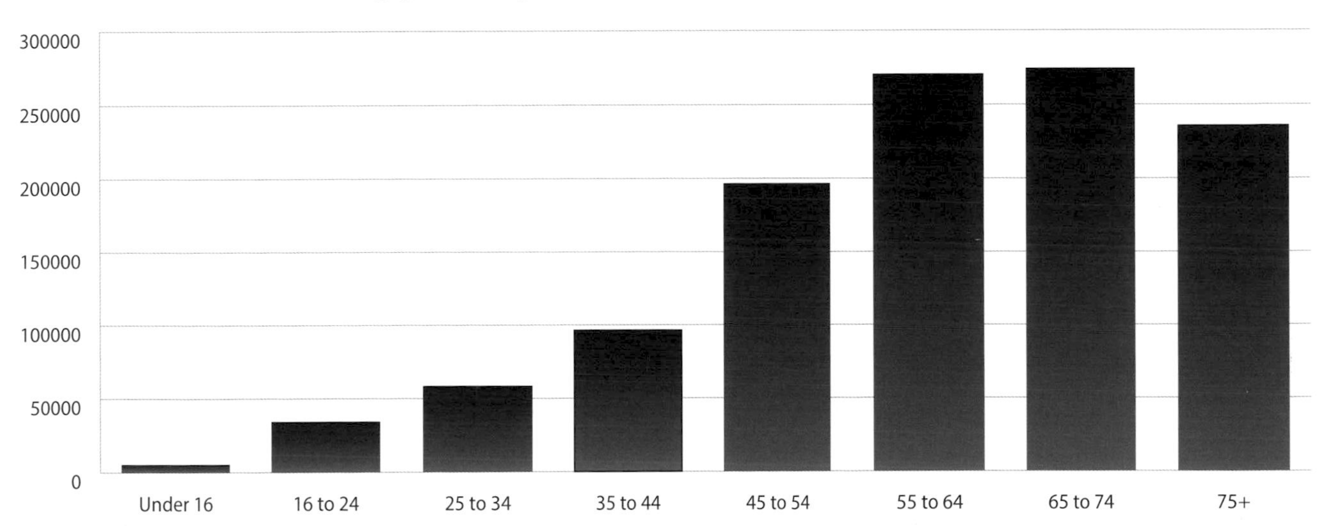

Source: Source: NHS Digital (2018) Statistics on Alcohol England

Chart 4.16: Hospital admissions for alcohol-related conditions per 100,000 population, 10-17 and 18-24 year olds, England, 2006/7 to 2015/16

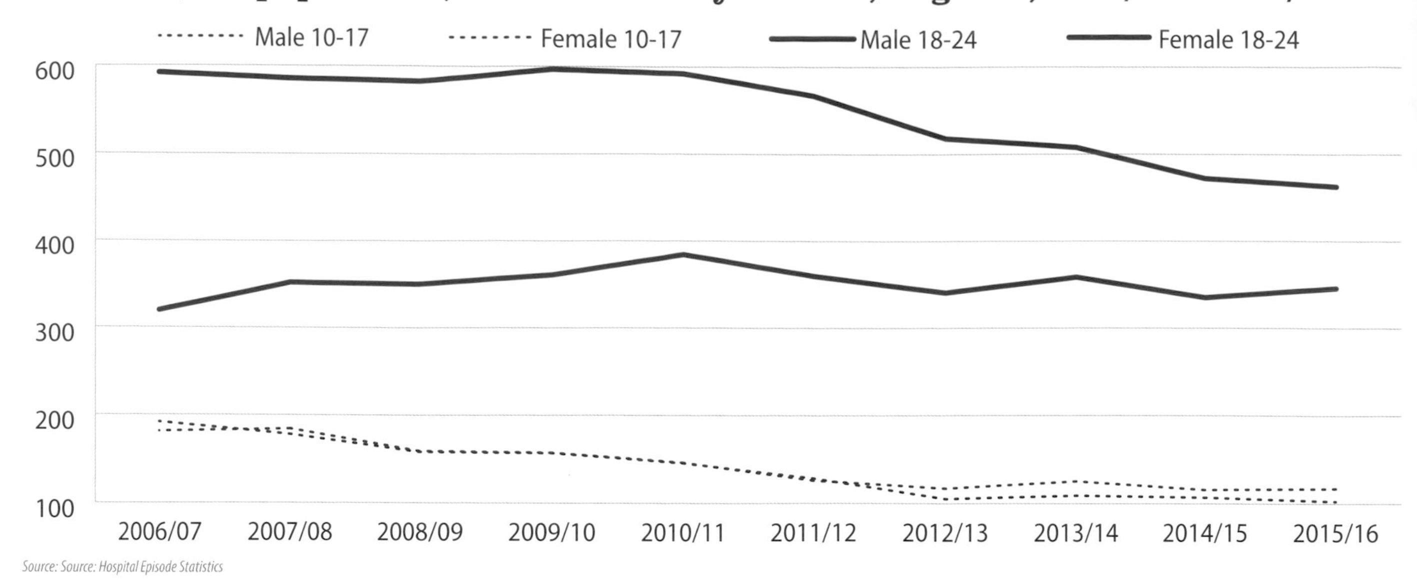

Source: Source: Hospital Episode Statistics

people who drank alcohol were more likely to drink alcohol themselves (NHS Digital, 2017).

Turning to older teenagers and young adults, higher proportions drink compared with the younger group. The latest Health Survey for England reported that the proportion of young people aged 16-25 who had not drunk in the last year was around one in five (22%), although the questions are not directly comparable to those used in surveys with the younger age group. A significant minority of young people (20% of young men and 13% of young women age 16-25) reported drinking in the risk categories (NHS Digital, 2018a).

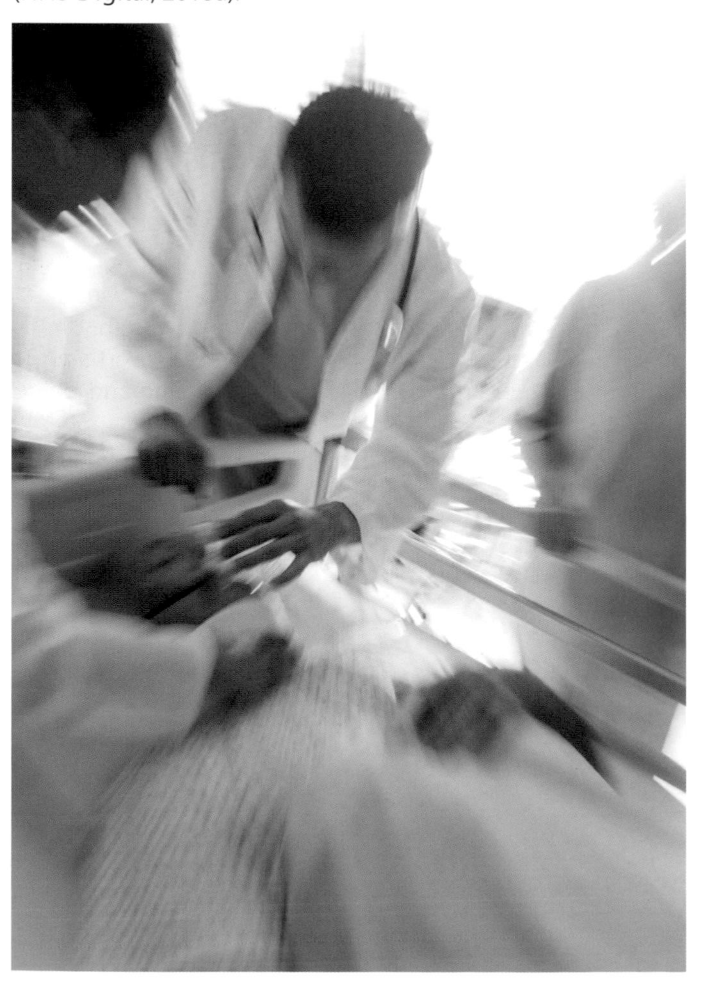

The trend has been for a decline in drinking in this older age group aged 16+, mirroring the pattern for secondary school pupils. The Health Survey for England 2016 survey showed that the pattern for heavier drinkers (more than 14 units per week) between 2011 and 2017 is less clear, as is shown in Chart 4.14.

Although drinking in young people is a serious concern because of the long-term health consequences and development of lifetime health habits, they are rarely hospitalised for alcohol related reasons when compared with other age groups. Chart 4.15 presents Hospital Episode Statistics (HES) for alcohol related admissions, illustrating the admissions pattern across the full population age range. Young people under 25 represent a very small proportion of all these admissions. By using data relating to the primary and secondary reason for admission, this ensures the data capture all admissions that are alcohol related including, for example, accidents.

Although rates of hospitalisation of young people for alcohol related conditions are low in absolute terms, the trends are not straightforward. Chart 4.16 compares the long-term trends for 10-17 year olds and 18-24 year olds. While rates have gone down for males aged 18-24 and for 10-17 year olds of both genders, young women aged 18-24 have not shown a decline.

2019

Heavier social media use linked to more frequent drinking in young people

Heavier social media use is associated with more frequent alcohol consumption among young people in the UK, according to a new UCL study.

Published today in the journal *Addiction*, the study found that those aged 10–15 who used social media more regularly were more likely to drink alcohol. The researchers also found a link between heavier social media use and more frequent binge drinking among young adults aged 16–19.

The study authors believe that this study is the first of its kind in the UK to show that this strong correlation exists, and that this relationship also occurs across time.

Researchers analysed data from the UK Household Longitudinal Study (Understanding Society), collected between 2011 and 2013 on 6,782 participants, and then followed-up in 2014 to 2016 with 3,645 participants. Study respondents were grouped into two age groups, 10–15 and 16–19, and self-reported their social media usage via self-completion questionnaires filled in private, administered by trained interviewers in participants' households.

Social media use was measured by asking how many hours respondents spent chatting or interacting with friends through social websites (including Facebook, Myspace and Bebo) on a normal weekday, with categories comprising 'no profile', 'non-daily use', 'less than an hour use per day', 'one to three hours' use per day', and 'four hours' use or more per day'. Drinking frequency was categorised as 'never', 'one to two times in the past month' and 'more than three times in the past month'. Binge drinking frequency was based on how many times participants aged 16–19-year-olds had drunk five or more drinks on a single occasion in the past month.

The study found that 18% of participants aged 10–15-years drank at least monthly, with a greater risk of more frequent drinking for each additional hour of social media use. Researchers found this association even when taking a range of factors into account such as sex, number of close friends, life satisfaction, rural or urban location and household income.

Among 10–15-year-olds, those with no social media profile, non-daily users and those who used social media for less than an hour a day were found to be less likely to drink at least monthly compared to those with one to three hours' use and over four hours' use. Compared to those who limited their social media use to less than an hour a day, those who used social media for four hours or more per day were more likely to drink once a month or more (42% vs 19%). They were also more likely to be female (64% vs 36%) and to be dissatisfied with their lives (13% vs 3%).

Looking at comparisons over time, the researchers found that among those aged 10–15 years, 43% increased their drinking frequency over the study period, with those who increased their social media use also more likely to drink more frequently.

Overall, the study found that 30% of respondents aged 16–19 drank at least weekly, also revealing a higher risk of binge drinking for those in this age group who used social media for four hours or more per day compared to those with less than an hour's use per day.

Study lead author Dr Linda Ng Fat (UCL Department of Epidemiology and Public Health) said: 'With a decline in alcohol consumption and a rise in social media use amongst young people around the world, we wanted to understand if and how social media use might be influencing how frequently young people drink. Our results indicate that social media is not directly behind this decline in alcohol consumption, and in fact highlights the positive link between social media use and drinking for both age groups in the study.

'However, the exact reasoning behind the association is not yet known. Given the recent rise in the number of social media platforms such as Snapchat, Instagram and TikTok - which weren't included in this study - it's vital that greater attention is paid to this issue so we can better understand the intricacies of this relationship.'

Study co-author Professor Yvonne Kelly (UCL Department of Epidemiology and Public Health) said: 'Experimentation with drinking during adolescence is all part and parcel of growing up. However, the pattern between time spent online and drinking among 10–15-year-olds in our study is particularly striking, given that the purchase of alcohol for this group is illegal, coupled with the potential problems associated with the introduction to alcohol from an earlier age.

'The reasons why time spent online could link to drinking behaviours are not clear but could include having negative experiences in online spaces, as well as exposure to advertising. Further research that builds on our study findings is key to understanding how time spent on social media platforms could be influencing the drinking habits of young people - either directly through alcohol advertising or indirectly through the normalisation of drinking and being drunk.'

The authors note that there are several limitations to their study; social media use was measured only in regard to chatting and interacting on a weekday, with passive use excluded, whilst alcohol consumption measures did not take volume into account. The authors also note that further research is required to understand the mechanisms behind the link between social media use and alcohol consumption and cannot state that this link is causal.

22 April 2021

Alcohol adverts 'commonly appeal' to underage teenagers, study finds

Researchers say the findings indicate potential 'weaknesses in the regulatory codes'.

By Erin Santillo & Josie Clarke

Adverts for alcohol 'commonly appeal' to teenagers under the legal drinking age, a study has found.

A survey of 11 to 17-year-olds by the Institute of Alcohol Studies (IAS) found just over half reacted positively to adverts featuring Fosters Radler beer and Smirnoff vodka brands (53% and 52% respectively), and a third (34%) reacted positively to an advert featuring the Haig Club whisky brand.

The findings, published in the journal *Alcohol and Alcoholism*, have led the IAS to call on UK policymakers to consider tighter alcohol advertising legislation, saying the research identifies potential 'weaknesses in the regulatory codes'.

Among approximately 1,500 adolescents who had never drunk alcohol, having a positive reaction to each of the adverts was associated with around one and a half times increased odds of being susceptible to drink in the next year.

And among approximately 900 current drinkers, positive reactions to two of the three adverts were associated with around 1.4 times increased odds of being a higher risk drinker.

Researchers said that while the study did not set out to prove a causal link between reactions to the adverts and alcohol use, the findings tied in with other evidence that had established underage adolescents' awareness of alcohol marketing as well as links between marketing exposure and subsequent alcohol use.

The IAS said that although only three adverts were used in the study, they were not in breach of the UK marketing codes and were therefore typical of alcohol advertising.

It concluded that 'in that light, the finding that these adverts commonly appealed to underage adolescents indicates there may be weaknesses in the regulatory codes themselves, their implementation, or both, and ultimately contributes to wider concerns about complaints-led self-regulatory approaches'.

Head of research at the IAS and lead author of the study, Dr Sadie Boniface, said: 'We already knew that exposure to alcohol marketing is high among young people.

'We wanted to build on other studies that spoke directly to young people about their views, taking advantage of the large number of adolescents in this study.

'Based on what we know from other research, it was not a surprise that these adverts commonly appealed to young people.

'The association between positive reactions to the adverts and being susceptible to drink among underage adolescents who have never tried alcohol.

'This was consistent for each of the three adverts studied.

'Taken together with other research, there is strong evidence the current UK alcohol marketing regulations are inadequate in protecting young people from being exposed to content that does appeal to them and influences their behaviour.'

The researchers analysed the responses of 2,500 people aged 11 to 17 in the Youth Alcohol Policy Survey conducted by YouGov for Cancer Research UK in April and May 2017.

23 April 2021

Are 'soap operas' driving young people to drink?

By Alex Barker

There is strong evidence to suggest that exposure to alcohol content or advertising in the media increases uptake and use in adolescents. Alcohol content in the media normalises these behaviours for young people, and young people may imitate behaviours of influential others, such as celebrities.

In the UK, TV programmes are regulated by the Ofcom Broadcasting Code which protects under-18s by restricting alcohol use in programmes made for children and preventing the glamorisation of alcohol use in programmes broadcast before the 9pm watershed or in programmes likely to be viewed by children. Furthermore, 'paid-for' product placement of alcohol products is prohibited.

Despite this, alcohol content is widely shown on TV, and our previous research, looking at alcohol content on television, identified that soap operas, or 'soaps', contained a lot of alcohol content, and are shown before the 9pm watershed when children and young people are likely to be watching TV with their parents. We decided to investigate how much alcohol content is shown in soaps broadcast on UK TV and explore the amount of young people exposed to this content

In our study, tobacco and alcohol content in soap operas broadcast on UK television: a content analysis and population exposure, we recorded all episodes of six soap operas (*EastEnders, Coronation Street, Emmerdale, Hollyoaks, Home and Away*, and *Neighbours)* broadcast on UK television during three separate weeks in November and December 2018, and January 2019. We then recorded the amount and types of alcohol content using 1-minute interval coding, which involved recording any alcohol content shown during every 1-minute interval of the programme in the following categories; any alcohol content, actual alcohol use, implied alcohol use, alcohol paraphernalia (such as beer pumps and bottles), and alcohol branding.

We found alcohol content was extremely common, occurring in 95% of the 87 episodes we coded, and in almost a quarter (24%) of 1-minute intervals from soaps (2,222 in total). Alcohol use was seen in 5% of intervals, most often involving beer or cider (three intervals depicted use by a person under the age of 18), implied use was seen in 14% of intervals, with people holding a drink being the most common occurrence, paraphernalia was seen in 18% of intervals, mostly involving beer pumps or bottles, and branding was seen in 5% of intervals, occurring exclusively through beer pumps or labels on bottles. Overall, 45 brands were seen, 30 were genuine branded alcohol products, 15 were fictional. The most commonly seen brand was 'Makers Mark'.

Interestingly, the two Australian soaps included in our study contained a lower proportion of intervals containing alcohol content compared to UK soaps. Genuine branded alcohol products were only seen in UK soaps.

To estimate the number of young people exposed to this content, we obtained viewing figures and used population estimates combined with alcohol appearances to estimate the number of impressions (number of times alcohol content was seen by a people in that age group). We estimate that the 87 soap episodes delivered 2.1 billion alcohol gross impressions (95% confidence interval [CI] 1.9–2.2) to the UK population, including 113 million (95% CI 99–127) to children aged under 16. There were 568 million (95% CI 534–602) gross impressions of branded alcohol products, including 26.62 million to children (95% CI 23.31–29.92).

Our study shows that soaps broadcast on UK TV are a significant source of exposure to alcohol imagery, including genuine alcohol branding to young people. And current alcohol regulations are failing to prevent a substantial degree of generic and branded exposure. Soaps are likely to be contributing to the normalisation of drinking behaviours in young and future generations, and it is likely that the high occurrence of alcohol use will drive alcohol consumption among young people. This is especially so in relation to branding, with these programmes delivering approximately 600 million branded alcohol impressions to the UK population, including 26 million to children under the age of 16. Whilst Ofcom prohibits paid-for alcohol product placement, programme makers can use 'props' (items which they do not receive payment for using) or fictional brands. We noticed that genuine brands were shown in programmes alongside fictional brands, calling into question why genuine alcohol brands are being used in scenes.

Furthermore, many of the brands featured in these programmes are not popular in the UK, with the most prominent brand, 'Maker's Mark', not appearing in a YouGov list of the most popular alcohol brands. The inclusion of these brands in UK soap operas is thus unjustifiable on the grounds of reflecting everyday life.

Tighter scheduling rules, such as showing these programmes after the 9pm watershed or following the example of the Australian soap operas and reducing the reliance on alcohol imagery, could prevent children and adolescents being exposed to this content.

The term 'soap opera' originates from the 1930s when daytime serial dramas on the radio were sponsored by soap production companies to advertise their products to housewives. Whilst paid-for alcohol product placement is prohibited, genuine alcohol brands receive widespread exposure from soaps broadcast on UK television. Ofcom should investigate the use of genuine brands in soaps to ensure that the use of these products complies with the broadcasting code.

14th July 2020

Why young people are drinking less – and what older drinkers can learn from them

An article from The Conversation.

THE CONVERSATION

By Dominic Conroy, Lecturer in Psychology, University of East London

Young people are drinking less than ever before. Some reading this will be able to recall the 1990s – the decade of peak alcohol, when drinking was a key part of life for young people. The decade saw the rise of pub and club culture, public displays of drunkenness by young adults and the arrival of new kinds of alcoholic drinks you could buy (alcopops anyone?).

Flash forward to 2020 and the picture is very different. A range of studies from countries where drinking is a big part of the culture confirms a sharp decline in alcohol consumption among young people. Research in Sweden, for example, shows a decline across all types of consumption, from the heaviest to the lightest drinkers. Similarly, rates of binge drinking have gone down and people defining themselves as non-drinkers has increased.

There may be significant health benefits to this change in behaviour. Excessive alcohol consumption is the cause of a number of chronic diseases and bad drinking habits are often created between the ages of 16 and 25. So there's lots to be learnt from the young people who typify how drinking culture appears to be changing.

There are many reasons for the change, which I have recently brought together in a new book with my colleague Fiona Measham. Economic factors, including a wider climate of constraint and austerity, may impinge the time and money young people have available to spend on alcohol. Young people may also be more aware of alcohol's health risks.

But changes in drinking behaviour may be just one part of broader changes in today's super-connected youth culture. For example, online technology has made friends and family now instantly accessible via social media and smartphones, and the once central role of pubs and clubs for initiating and consolidating social networks appears to have changed.

The decline could also simply be a redressing of the balance that began with the surge in alcohol's popularity during the 1990s. It is unclear what the definitive reason is for the change that has taken place. But there is still plenty to learn from these changes in terms of how to encourage others to adopt healthier drinking patterns.

Pros and cons of not drinking

Choosing not to drink alcohol can have implications for people's social lives. I carried out a study, surveying 500 UK university students who were alcohol drinkers but who were asked about whether they had recently not drunk alcohol on social occasions where their peers were drinking.

Nearly half (44%) of the students reported having socialised without drinking alcohol, and reported benefits including higher self-esteem and feeling more productive in life. The main downsides were concerns that not drinking might limit their social lives and fear of missing out. The high proportion of students who had abstained from social drinking in the previous week while in the company of alcohol-consuming friends suggests that going dry while socialising may be more widespread among young adults who do regularly consume alcohol than is typically acknowledged in popular culture.

Not drinking has gained cultural visibility in recent years with the rise of phenomena like Dry January. But questions circle around these initiatives. There is currently limited evidence that these events translate into longer-term moderate drinking and whether or not they target those in the most need of curbing their alcohol consumption is also open to question. So it seems we're still some way off harnessing non-drinking as a way to promote moderate alcohol consumption over a sustained period.

Beating the stigma

One of the biggest roadblocks to encouraging young people to drink less is the stigma there still is around not drinking or even drinking in moderation. Many studies point to this, particularly among students. In one study I worked on, interviewees have spoken of experiencing peer pressure to drink, and if they don't drink alcohol feeling like they 'don't belong' or even excluded.

Another study suggests that male non-drinkers may face a double whammy of stigma. Their decision to not drink clashes with expectations of being both a young person (where drinking to excess demonstrates 'living life to the full') and gender role specific expectations (being told: 'Why are you not having a drink? Man up!').

Nonetheless, we can expect to see a growth in tolerance toward different drinking behaviour, as more people decide to drink less. This may unlock all sorts of possibilities when it comes to promoting moderate drinking across the population at large. The rise in interest in drink-free challenges, for example, and healthier lifestyles more generally, suggests the cultural climate is ripe for putting non-drinking centre stage in public health promotion materials.

Also, the emergence of 'sober spaces' in young adult social environments is significant. For example, the rise of cafe culture, increased demand for living accommodation where alcohol use is prohibited and activities like sober raves and the 'conscious clubbing' movement. Pubs and clubs are no longer the go-to space for people to socialise, thanks to diverse cultural factors including increased numbers of young people who do not drink and the increased acceptability of non-drinking as a social option.

Understanding these changes is an ongoing process. But shifts in how alcohol is viewed by young adults shows that excessive drinking doesn't have to be the default way of socialising and perhaps we can all have a healthier relationship with booze.

10 March 2020

www.theconversation.com

Almost one in four young adults now teetotal, report reveals

Report discovers that one in three young adults have reduced alcohol consumption.

By Sabrina Barr

Almost a quarter of young adults have decided to completely forgo alcohol, a new report has discovered.

Every year, the Society of Independent Brewers (Siba) publishes a British craft beer report, analysing growing trends from within the craft beer sector.

In the latest report, which is due to be published on Thursday 12 March, the organisation found that an increasing number of young people are opting to drink beers with a lower alcohol content, while others have chosen to go teetotal.

According to the report's findings, 23 per cent of 18 to 24 year olds do not drink alcohol, marking an increase of six per cent over the past 12 months.

Meanwhile, the research outlined that there has been a 30 per cent rise in sales for no- or low-alcohol beers since 2016.

The burgeoning interest for no- or low-alcohol beverages has gained increasing prominence in the drinks market as of late.

Last July, Sainsbury's announced it would be opening the UK's first no- and low-alcohol pub in central London in the summer of 2020, following an 'exciting spike in the no- and low-alcohol category'.

A recent study conducted by the University of Sheffield concluded that abstinence rates among 16 to 24 year olds rose from 10 per cent to nearly 25 per cent between 2001 and 2016.

Neil Walker, spokesperson for Siba, stated that the popularity of drinking no- or low-alcohol beers is showing 'no signs of wavering'.

'Low or no-alcohol beers have never been better and some of the best examples are made by small independent breweries,' Mr Walker said.

'It's a trend that shows no signs of wavering and means that people who choose not to drink, are driving or just want to cut down, now have plenty of tasty options.'

James Grundy, co-founder of The Small Beer Brew Co, added that experiencing hangovers has become less 'desirable'.

'We know people enjoy walking through their front doors and transitioning from work to home with the opening of a beer,' Mr Grundy stated.

'But now people want that without the cloudy-headed morning after, as that slowdown is no longer a desirable part of people's lifestyles.'

In December, it was reported that a third of millennials in the UK were planning on hosting a teetotal Christmas.

11 March 2020

What to do when you are worried about your parent's drinking

By Piers Henriques

If your mum or dad is drinking too much alcohol, it is not always easy to know what to do or how you should be feeling about it. In this blog, Piers Henriques from Nacoa shares some top tips about what to do if you are worried about your parent's drinking and how to look after yourself.

What happens when a parent drinks too much?

The most important thing to know if you are worried about your parent's drinking is that you are not alone facing these issues. You are not to blame, you didn't cause it, and you can't control it. You can, however, take care of yourself, communicate your feelings, and make healthy choices.

If you have found this article, you may well be in the same situation as millions of others in the UK who are upset or worried about their parent's relationship with alcohol. The secrecy, shame and blame that goes round in these situations can make you feel really confused. That is why Nacoa UK exists, to create a space for this kind of information and support so you can feel better and live a happy, fulfilling life.

Though you may feel you are the only one, it is normal for children of alcohol-dependent parents to:

- Feel too embarrassed to take friends home
- Feel confused when your mum or dad change when they drink
- Feel nobody really cares what happens to you
- Feel guilty and don't know why
- Feel different from other people
- Keep secrets about problems in your family
- Tell lies to cover up for someone's drinking
- Believe no one could possibly understand how you feel

Your life can be hugely affected by your parent's drinking no matter how old you are, whether you live with them, or how 'successful' your family may look to the outside world. Take a look at Nacoa's Experiences pages to find hundreds of personal posts about the above points (and much more) from the Nacoa community.

People in this situation often describe themselves as a COA or ACOA (child of an alcoholic or adult child of an alcoholic). Putting a name on it can help you realise this is 'a thing'. Being a COA matters, no matter what anyone says, and you deserve help and support. That's why Nacoa UK is here for you.

What can I do?

Alcohol problems are often described as being like an illness where the person has lost control of their drinking and usually needs help to stop. There is help out there for them and you must remember that you can feel better if your parent continues to drink or not.

An alcohol problem in the family can become a taboo that no one wants to talks about. But even if your family is not ready to speak about it, looking after yourself will help you feel better:

- **Remember you are not responsible for other people's drinking** – You can't control someone else's drinking or behaviour. Pouring away, watering down or hiding alcohol may make things worse, and the person drinking may become angry, upset or secretive.
- **Remember alcohol affects the brain** – Alcohol can make people forget things. They often don't remember silly, embarrassing or other things they have done. Try not to argue with your parents when they've been drinking.
- **Be realistic** – When someone has a drink problem, alcohol often becomes their main priority. The need to drink becomes so important that they may hurt and upset people they love.
- **Your mum or dad can only stop drinking when they are ready** – There is help available, but they have to accept that they have a problem and want to stop. It is not your responsibility to stop your parent drinking. It is important to look after yourself.

How can I feel better?

It is often the case that children of alcohol-dependent parents feel overwhelmed with a desire to help their parents stop drinking. Sometimes people stage what is called an 'intervention', where friends or family will confront the drinking parent and encourage them to acknowledge their problem. Or sometimes a medical professional or social welfare practitioner might become involved by request.

People's children can be hugely important to those who find help with an addiction. However, it is vital for you as the child of that person to know that the success of their treatment is not your responsibility in any way. You are not a failure if your parent continues to drink.

Regardless of whether mum or dad continue to drink, you can find help and feel better.

- **Talk to someone you trust** – It is not being disloyal to speak to a friend, relative, a teacher, or Nacoa, to talk about the problems you face. Sharing feelings can help you feel less alone. Nacoa promises to listen and not judge.
- **Make time for yourself** – Whether it's sports, arts, or hobbies, taking a break can help you feel less stressed and more connected to others outside of your family. This is your life, too.
- **Understand that your feelings are normal** – It's okay to hate the problems that alcohol problems cause yet love the person who is drinking. It is important to externalise your own experiences and emotions. You can share with likeminded people on the moderated Nacoa message boards or keep a journal. Some people write letters, then tear them up. It helps!
- **Read and watch things about the problem** – The Nacoa website has hundreds of Experience pieces written by other COAs. We also list books and films that help you to realise that, even though you might feel isolated, millions of people around the world face this problem.
- **Find services that can help** – Alanon/Alateen, Adfam, and Nacoa have amazing resources for you to find and use for free. It is an act of bravery and strength to reach out for help. So find what works for you from available services and charities. Think of finding advice and support as if you are making individual steps rather than one huge leap.

Above anything else, please remember: You are not to blame, you didn't cause it, and you can't control it. You can, though, take care of yourself, communicate your feelings, and make healthy choices. You are not alone.

Nacoa (The National Association for Children of Alcoholics) provides information, advice and support for everyone affected by a parent's drinking. Check out Nacoa.org.uk to find more about the free phone and email helpline, online message boards, and hundreds of experience posts from their community of supporters and professionals.

29 June 2021

Key Facts

- There is no completely safe level of drinking. (page 2)
- Alcohol and the compounds that alcohol is broken down into by your liver are poisonous and although they are eventually excreted from the system, they have a potentially damaging effect on almost every system of the body, which can result in health damage over time. (page 3)
- The scientific name for the alcohol in drinks is ethanol or ethyl alcohol. (page 3)
- People who are more dependent on alcohol may have withdrawal symptoms if they stop drinking suddenly and these can be severe. (page 4)
- Anyone over 18 can buy and drink alcohol legally in licensed premises in Britain. (page 4)
- In 2019, there were 7,565 deaths registered in the UK that related to alcohol-specific causes, the second highest since the data time series began in 2001. (page 5)
- Since the beginning of the data time series in 2001, rates of alcohol-specific deaths for males have consistently been more than double those for females (16.1 and 7.8 deaths per 100,000 registered in 2019 respectively). (page 5)
- Northern Ireland and Scotland had the highest rates of alcohol-specific death in 2019 (18.8 and 18.6 deaths per 100,000 people respectively). (page 5)
- Rates of male alcohol-specific deaths are twice those of females. (page 5)
- The majority of alcohol-specific deaths are attributed to alcoholic liver disease. (page 5)
- Alcohol can cause 7 different types of cancer. (page 8)
- Breast cancer is the most common cancer in the UK and drinking alcohol is one of the biggest risk factors for breast cancer. (page 9)
- Nearly a third of people (29%) are reporting that they have drunk more alcohol than they normally would during COVID-19 lockdown. (page 10)
- Alcohol is addictive both psychologically and physically. (page 10)
- Regularly drinking more than 14 units of alcohol a week risks damaging your health. (page 12)
- The NHS says alcohol misuse is when you drink in any way that's harmful, or when you're dependent on alcohol. (page 18)
- One study, published in 2004, estimated there were about 3,000 to 4,000 suspected drink spiking incidents a year in Australia. It estimated less than 15% of incidents were reported to police. (page 20)
- Four out of five victims of drink spiking were women. (page 21)
- Drink-driving is one of the biggest killers on our roads. (page 22)
- In the UK if a driver is found to be over the drink-drive limit, and/or driving while impaired by alcohol, they can receive a maximum penalty of six months in prison, an unlimited fine and an automatic driving ban of at least one year. (page 22)
- Nine in ten North-East children aged 15 or younger are not drinking regularly. (page 25)
- One in three teenagers who drink are drinking more since the start of the pandemic. (page 25)
- Children and their parents and carers are advised that an alcohol-free childhood is the healthiest and best option. (page 26)
- It's against the law to drive with more than 80mg (milligrams) alcohol per 100ml (millilitres) of blood, or 50mg in Scotland. (page 27)
- Parents are now the main providers of alcohol for teenagers (70%). (page 27)
- 55% of Brits had tried alcohol for the first time by the time they turned 15. (page 28)
- One in four (25%) Brits say they had tried alcohol well before legal age, at 13 or younger. (page 28)
- Younger adults are more likely to be lenient with their children and drinking, for example 22% of 18 to 24 year olds would let their children have spirits at age 16, compared to only 9% of over 65s who say the same. (page 29)
- Pupils who lived with people who drank alcohol were more likely to drink alcohol themselves. (page 30-32)
- Those aged 10-15 who used social media more regularly were more likely to drink alcohol. (page 33)
- Among approximately 1,500 adolescents who had never drunk alcohol, having a positive reaction to each of the adverts was associated with around one and a half times increased odds of being susceptible to drink in the next year. (page 34)
- Soap operas deliver approximately 600 million branded alcohol impressions to the UK population, including 26 million to children under the age of 16. (page 35)
- In a survey of 500 University students nearly half (44%) of the students reported having socialised without drinking alcohol, and reported benefits including higher self-esteem and feeling more productive in life. (page 36)
- Almost a quarter of young adults have decided to completely forgo alcohol, a new report has discovered. (page 37)

Glossary

Addiction
A dependence on a substance which makes it very difficult to stop taking it. Addiction can be either physical, meaning the user's body has become dependent on the substance and will suffer negative symptoms if the substance is withdrawn, or psychological, meaning a user has no physical need to take a substance, but will experience strong cravings if it is withdrawn.

Alcohol
The type of alcohol found in drinks, ethanol, is an organic compound. The ethanol in alcoholic beverages such as wine and beer is produced through the fermentation of plants containing carbohydrates. Ethanol can cause intoxication if drunk excessively.

Alcohol By Volume (ABV)
ABV is a measure of how much pure alcohol is present in a drink. It is represented as a percentage of the total volume of the drink. For example, a one-litre bottle of an alcoholic beverage will provide an ABV value on its label. This informs the buyer what percentage of that one litre consists of pure alcohol.

Alcohol dependency/alcoholism
Alcohol is a drug and it is addictive. If someone becomes dependent on drink to the extent that they feel they need it just to get through the day, they may be referred to as an alcoholic. In addition to the various health problems related to alcoholism, an alcoholic`s relationships and career may also suffer due to their addiction. They can suffer withdrawal symptoms if they don`t drink alcohol regularly and may need professional help from an organisation such as Alcoholics Anonymous to deal with their dependency.

Binge drinking
When an individual consumes large quantities of alcohol in one session, usually with the intention of becoming drunk, this is popularly referred to as 'binge drinking'. It is widely accepted that drinking four or more drinks in a short space of time constitutes 'bingeing', and this can have severe negative effects on people's health.

Depressant
A substance that slows down the nervous system, making the user feel calmer and more relaxed. These drugs are also known as 'downers' and include alcohol, heroin and tranquillisers.

Detox
Ridding the body of toxins, i.e. drugs.

Drink-driving
Drink-driving is being in charge of, or driving, a motor vehicle, or attempting to, whilst under the influence of alcohol.

Drink spiking
When someone adds alcohol or drugs to another person`s drink without their knowledge or consent, it is said that their drink has been `spiked`. Drink spiking is sometimes, but not always, done in order to facilitate another crime such as rape or assault. Prevention strategies include using a `stopper` in the tops of bottles to prevent anything being added to the drink, and never leaving a drink alone.

Hangover
A hangover describes the effects of alcohol the day after intoxication. Alcohol is a depressant, causes the body to dehydrate and also irritates the stomach, so hangovers usually involve a severe headache, nausea, diarrhoea, a depressive mood and tiredness. There are many myths about how to cure a hangover but the only real solution is to drink plenty of water and wait for it to pass – or of course to drink less alcohol in the first place!

Intoxication
The state of being drunk, caused by drinking too much alcohol. Drunkenness can lead to dizziness, sickness, loss of memory, aggression or anti-social behaviour, as well as potentially causing long-term health problems such as cirrhosis of the liver. Due to the loss of inhibitions associated with heavy alcohol use, it can also cause people to indulge in risk-taking behaviour they would not normally consider – for example, having unprotected sex.

Teetotal
A teetotaller is someone who abstains completely from alcohol. If an individual is trying to recover from an alcohol dependency they will usually be teetotal. However, people abstain from drinking for many other reasons, including religion, pregnancy, for health reasons or just through personal preference.

Unit of alcohol
The unit system is a method used to measure the strength of an alcoholic drink. One unit is 10ml of pure alcohol – the amount of alcohol the average adult can process within the space of one hour. Units can be calculated by multiplying the amount of alcohol in millilitres by the drink's ABV, and dividing by 1,000.

Activities

Brainstorming

- In small groups discuss what you know about alcohol.
  - What types of alcohol are there?
  - What problems can alcohol misuse cause?
  - What are the health risks involved in drinking too much?

Research

- Do some research into the types of cancer alcohol consumption might cause. Produce an infographic to show your findings.
- Research alcohol abuse and the effects it can have on a person. What are the risks involved in excessive drinking? Write a two-page report on your findings.
- Talk to friends about their alcohol consumption and find out if they drink and if so, the reasons why they drink.
- In pairs, do some research into children who live with alcoholic parents. How does this impact on their lives? Is this likely to lead them to become drinkers? Share your findings with the rest of your class.
- Do some research on the types of alcohol that people may drink. Are there any drinks that appeal to some age groups/genders more than others?
- In small groups, research the effects that alcohol have on the brain and body. Present your findings on a poster.
- In small groups, do some research on sponsorship by alcohol companies. Do they sponsor any television programmes or sports teams? Or do you see adverts on social media?
- In pairs, research how many drink-driving deaths there are each year. Present your findings in an infographic.

Design

- Create a leaflet which raises awareness about the dangers surrounding excessive drinking. It should list some of the organisations which could be of help as well as practical advice.
- Design a poster to be displayed in schools, which highlights the risks of drinking too much as a teenager. It should be informative and list the potential health problems and risky behaviours which can occur through excessive drinking and the long-term implications to their lives.
- Design an illustration to highlight the key themes/messages of one of the articles in this book.
- In pairs, create a reel to explain the dangers of drinking.
- In small groups, create a campaign to raise the awareness of drink-spiking. Make sure you include ways to keep safe and how spot the signs.
- Design a poster on drink-driving.
- Design a signposting poster for people seeking help on alcohol abuse.

Oral

- Have a class discussion about drinking amongst teenagers and the risks to them. Discuss ways in which you think these issues could be addressed.
- In small groups, prepare a presentation that explains the health risks of drinking. Share your findings with your class.
- Split the class into two groups. One group will argue in favour of alcohol sponsorship of television programmes and the other group will argue against.
- In pairs, go through this topic and discuss the cartoons you come across. Think about what the artists were trying to portray with each illustration.
- In pairs, stage a discussion between two friends where one of you is trying to persuade the other to give up drinking. Take it in turns to play the role of the persuader.

Reading/writing

- Imagine you are an Agony Aunt writing for a national newspaper. A teen has written to you as they are living with an alcoholic parent. Their parent becomes argumentative and sometimes violent. Write a suitable reply giving advice and information on where they may look for support and help.
- Write a one-paragraph definition of 'alcohol abuse' and compare it with a classmate's.
- Write a blog about binge-drinking in the under-16s and explain why teenagers should not drink at such a young age.
- Choose an article from the book and write a summary of it. This should be at least two paragraphs long.
- Can you think of a film or book where a character struggles with alcohol abuse? Write a short review of it.

Index

Acknowledgements

The publisher is grateful for permission to reproduce the material in this book. While every care has been taken to trace and acknowledge copyright, the publisher tenders its apology for any accidental infringement or where copyright has proved untraceable. The publisher would be pleased to come to a suitable arrangement in any such case with the rightful owner.

The material reproduced in *ISSUES* books is provided as an educational resource only. The views, opinions and information contained within reprinted material in *ISSUES* books do not necessarily represent those of Independence Educational Publishers and its employees.

Images

Cover image courtesy of iStock. All other images courtesy of Freepik, Pixabay and Unsplash.

Illustrations

Simon Kneebone: pages 11, 15 & 38. Angelo Madrid: pages 2, 12 & 31.

Additional acknowledgements

Page 8: Cancer Research UK, https://www.cancerresearchuk.org/about-cancer/causes-of-cancer/alcohol-and-cancer/does-alcohol-cause-cancer, Accessed June 2021.

With thanks to the Independence team: Shelley Baldry, Danielle Lobban and Jackie Staines.

Tracy Biram

Cambridge, September 2021